FORTRESS OF JUSTIFICATION
A FRESH LOOK AT ROMANS

JAMES J. BURKE

FIREPROOF
COMMENTARIES

FIREPROOF COMMENTARIES

VOLUME V

ISBN-13: 979-8-9941637-8-8

All Scripture quotations are taken from the King James Version of the Bible unless otherwise indicated.

Printed in the United States of America
fireproofcommentaries.org

Table of Contents

How to Read This Book

Fortress of Justification is not written as a devotional, a reference manual, or a systematic theology. It is a guided walk through the argument of the Apostle Paul in the Epistle to the Romans.

Paul does not merely state conclusions in Romans; he builds them. Each section prepares the ground for the next, removing false securities before offering true refuge. This book follows that same order deliberately. To read it well is to allow the structure to stand as it is assembled.

Read Sequentially

The chapters are meant to be read in order. Early sections may feel severe or unsettling, especially as Paul exposes sin, judgment, and human accountability. That discomfort is intentional. Romans cannot be understood by leaping ahead to comfort before the problem has been fully established.

Skipping ahead weakens the force of what follows. Assurance rests securely only when it is built on truth that has been allowed to do its full work.

Attend to the Metaphors

The architectural language of gatehouse, drawbridge, road, walls, and fortress is not decorative. It is explanatory. These images are meant to help the reader see Paul's logic as a unified structure rather than a collection of isolated doctrines.

Let the metaphors guide you, but always allow Scripture itself to remain primary.

Do Not Rush the Cross

Romans delays explicit discussion of the cross and justification longer than many modern readers expect. This is not an oversight. Paul withholds relief until every false confidence has collapsed. When Christ's saving work is finally revealed, it arrives not as an abstract doctrine but as the only refuge God has provided.

Trust the delay. It is part of the mercy of the argument.

Use the Appendices as Support, Not Detours

The appendices exist to clarify concepts that could distract from the main flow if explained inline. They are not side debates, nor are they required reading on a first pass.

If a question arises—about God's righteousness, divine wrath, judgment according to works, or the order of Paul's argument—the appendices are there to steady the structure, not to replace it.

Read as One Who Is Being Addressed

Romans is not written to observers. It addresses Jews and Gentiles, the irreligious and the religious, the confident and the anxious. This book follows Paul in refusing to let the reader stand at a safe distance.

Read with openness. Allow the text to confront before it comforts, to accuse before it assures, and to dismantle before it builds.

The goal of this book is not merely understanding, but rest—rest grounded in the righteousness of God, secured by the work of Christ, and inhabited by a people who no longer stand on performance, heritage, or comparison.

Read patiently. The fortress is worth the walk.

Preface

The book of Romans is often approached as a grand cathedral of theology—towering, ornate, and perhaps a bit intimidating to the casual traveler. We look at its complex arguments on law, grace, and election as if they were stained glass: beautiful to observe from a distance, but difficult to touch. Yet, when Paul wrote this letter to the house churches of Rome, he wasn't merely delivering an abstract lecture. He was engaged in construction.

He was building a "fortress".

The title of this volume, Fortress of Justification, reflects the specific reality of the Roman church in the first century. It was a community under immense pressure—not just from the looming shadow of the Empire, but from the internal fractures of its own making. Jewish and Gentile believers were struggling to navigate their shared identity, often falling back into the worldly "patronage system" of earned status and social hierarchy.

Into this tension, Paul speaks a word that levels every human height. He declares a righteousness that cannot be earned, a standing that cannot be lost, and a peace that surpasses the power of any Caesar. Justification is not just a legal term; it is the bedrock of a new way of being human together.

In this commentary, we will walk through the "Gatehouse" of the gospel in Chapter 1, cross the "Drawbridge of Faith" in Chapter 3, and eventually find ourselves resting within the "Inner Keep" of God's sovereign love in Chapter 8. My goal is not to offer a new or novel interpretation, but to provide a "fresh look" that helps the modern reader see Romans as Paul intended: as a practical, life-sustaining stronghold.

Whether you are a student of the Word seeking depth or a weary traveler looking for solid ground, it is my prayer that these pages help you see the finished architecture of God's grace. May you find that in Christ, you are not merely "safe"—you are secure within the Fortress of Justification.

— James J. Burke

Marinette, Wisconsin

2026

Introduction

Introduction: The Stronghold of God

In the middle of the first century, Rome was not merely a city; it was the nerve center of the known world. From its marble heart flowed the law, military might, and cultural gravity that bound distant provinces to the capital. To speak to Rome was to speak to the empire itself.

Yet, for all its grandeur, Rome was a city of rigid, unyielding social structures. One's standing—legal, ethnic, and economic—was the currency of daily life. It was a world governed by the patronage system, a complex web of "who you know" and "what you are owed". Status was not just a preference; it was a fortress of privilege that determined who was protected and who was discarded. It is into this world of tiered humanity that the gospel of Jesus Christ quietly arrived.

Judea, Jews, and the Roman Seed

The church in Rome likely began not through a formal apostolic mission, but through Jewish believers returning from Pentecost in Jerusalem. These earliest Roman Christians were deeply shaped by the Hebrew Scriptures and the expectation of a Messiah. For years, the church was Jewish in character, understanding the gospel through the familiar categories of the law, the prophets, and the covenant.

The Expulsion and the Gentile Shift

Around A.D. 49, the ground shifted. Emperor Claudius expelled the Jews from Rome. While the decree was political, its impact on the church was seismic: the original Jewish leadership and the church's "cultural memory" were forcibly removed overnight.

For five years, the church in Rome existed almost entirely as a Gentile congregation. In the absence of Jewish influence, the "habits of the church" naturally evolved. Dietary concerns disappeared from the communal table, and the rhythm of feast days faded. The Gentiles learned to follow Christ without the scaffolding of the Mosaic Law. When Nero allowed the Jews to return in A.D. 54, they did not find the church they had left.

The returning Jewish believers expected to resume their roles as the "older brothers" of the faith, while the Gentiles—now the established leaders—saw no reason to return to "Jewish" ways. What had once been a shared faith now felt like competing claims to legitimacy.

The Question of Standing

The conflict in Rome was about more than food or calendars; it was a battle over standing. The church was inadvertently importing the Roman patronage system into the kingdom of God. They were trying to determine who had the "stronger claim" on God's favor.

They were rebuilding inside the church the very walls Christ had come to dismantle: a hierarchy of righteousness.

Why Paul Writes Romans

Paul writes this letter into this specific tension—not to arbitrate minor customs, but to redefine standing from the ground up. He does not appeal to Jewish heritage or Gentile freedom; instead, he points to a gospel that levels all human pride.

He writes to show that in Christ, the Roman system of "earned status" is dead. Whether you were a prestigious Roman citizen or a returning Jewish exile, your standing before God is identical: you are a sinner justified by grace alone.

A church at the center of the world could not afford a fragile, divided gospel. It needed a foundation strong enough to hold Jew and Gentile together under the crushing weight of imperial pressure. What follows is not an abstract theological lecture. It is construction. Paul is building a Fortress of Justification—a structure of truth where every believer, regardless of their past or their pedigree, can stand secure in the peace of God.

1

The Gatehouse of the Gospel

Paul, a servant of Jesus Christ, called to be an apostle, separated unto the gospel of God,

(Which he had promised afore by his prophets in the holy scriptures,)

Concerning his Son Jesus Christ our Lord, which was made of the seed of David according to the flesh;

And declared to be the Son of God with power, according to the spirit of holiness, by the resurrection from the dead:

By whom we have received grace and apostleship, for obedience to the faith among all nations, for his name:

Among whom are ye also the called of Jesus Christ:

To all that be in Rome, beloved of God, called to be saints: Grace to you and peace from God our Father, and the Lord Jesus Christ. (Romans 1:1-7)

Every fortress has a gate. It is the place where authority is declared, identity is established, and access is defined. Before any walls rise, before any ground is secured, the question must be answered: Who may enter, and on what terms?

Romans begins here.

Paul does not open his letter by addressing the conflict in Rome directly. He does something far more foundational. In seven verses, he names the Lord of the fortress, defines the gospel that grants entry, and identifies the people who belong inside. The church in Rome is divided not over Christ's identity, but over what qualifies a person to stand securely in Him. Nothing that follows can be understood apart from this opening declaration.

A Man Under Authority

"Paul, a servant of Jesus Christ, called to be an apostle, separated unto the gospel of God," *(Romans 1:1)*

Paul introduces himself with three titles, and their order is intentional.

First, he is a servant of Jesus Christ. Before Paul is a theologian, missionary, or church leader, he is owned. The word servant (*doulos*) denotes belonging, not employment. Paul does not speak on his own behalf, nor does he advance a personal agenda. He stands under authority.

Second, he is called to be an apostle. His authority is not derived from Rome, Jerusalem, or any congregation. It is the result of divine summons. Paul does not argue for his legitimacy; he assumes it, because his calling originates with Christ Himself.

Third, he is separated unto the gospel of God. Paul's life has been set apart not to a culture, a law, or a philosophical system, but to a *message*. And that message does not belong to Paul. It is the gospel of God—God's announcement, God's initiative, God's saving work.

The gatehouse opens with this truth: the gospel is not negotiable property controlled by the church. It is a divine proclamation delivered by a servant under orders.

A Gospel Rooted in Promise

(Which he had promised afore by his prophets in the holy scriptures,) (Romans 1:2)

Paul immediately anchors the gospel in continuity. Christianity is not a rupture from Israel's Scriptures but their fulfillment. The good news proclaimed by Paul is the same redemptive purpose God blueprinted long beforehand through the prophets.

This matters deeply for a divided church. The gospel does not belong exclusively to Jewish history nor does it bypass it. The same Scriptures that shaped Jewish expectation now testify to Christ for Jew and Gentile alike.

The gate is ancient. It was not installed recently.

A Gospel Concerning a Person

"Concerning his Son Jesus Christ our Lord..." (Romans 1:3–4)

Paul defines the gospel not as a theory but as a testimony concerning a Son.

First, Christ is presented in His true humanity and covenant lineage:

"Which was made of the seed of David according to the flesh;" (Romans 1:3)

Jesus is not a spiritual abstraction. He stands in the line of promise, the rightful heir to David's throne, fully participating in human history.

Second, Christ is declared in His divine authority and power:

"And declared to be the Son of God with power, according to the spirit of holiness, by the resurrection from the dead:" (Romans 1:4)

The resurrection is God's public verdict. It does not create Christ's sonship; it reveals it unmistakably. The crucified Jesus is vindicated as Lord. The fortress stands because its gate is guarded by a risen King.

Everything Paul will later say about justification rests here. A gospel without resurrection has no power to declare sinners righteous or to keep them secure.

Grace That Produces Allegiance

"By whom we have received grace and apostleship, for obedience to the faith among all nations, for his name:" (Romans 1:5)

Grace is not given merely to cancel guilt; it is given to establish rightful allegiance. Paul speaks of obedience to the faith, not obedience *as a substitute for faith.*

Faith, in Paul's usage, is not mere assent. It is trusting submission to Jesus Christ as Lord. Grace creates obedience because grace restores order—placing the believer back under God's rightful rule.

This obedience is not restricted by ethnicity or culture. It extends among all nations, because the Lordship of Christ knows no borders.

At the gatehouse, Paul makes something unmistakable: no one enters the fortress by heritage, and no one remains by self-direction.

A People Defined by Calling

"Among whom are ye also the called of Jesus Christ:"

"To all that be in Rome, beloved of God, called to be saints..." (Romans 1:6–7)

Paul now names the identity of those inside.

They are *called of Jesus Christ*—their faith is not accidental.

They are *beloved of God*—their standing is relational, not earned.

They are *called to be saints*—set apart, not superior.

This language strips away every competing claim to spiritual rank. Jewish believers cannot appeal to ancestry. Gentile believers cannot appeal to freedom. Both stand only because God has called them.

Paul closes the gatehouse declaration with the gospel's settled outcome:

> *"Grace to you and peace from God our Father, and the Lord Jesus Christ." (Romans 1:7)*

Grace is the ground. Peace is the wall. Where God grants righteousness, hostility is removed. Accusation loses its power.

Summary

Romans begins by establishing the unshakable foundation of the gospel.

Paul writes as a servant under Christ's authority, proclaiming a gospel promised in Scripture, centered on the risen Son of David, and effective among all nations. Entry into God's saving work is not determined by law, culture, or status, but by divine calling. Those who enter stand not on performance, but in grace—and are surrounded by peace with God.

Before Paul addresses sin, division, or judgment, he secures the gate.

Application

1. Examine what you are standing on.

   If Christ is the Door, nothing else can support your weight—heritage, sincerity, effort, or knowledge.

2. Receive grace as allegiance, not exemption.

   Grace does not free us from Christ's authority; it restores us to it.

3. Refuse every hierarchy Christ has dismantled.

   In the fortress of the gospel, all who enter stand on the same ground.

4. Rest in peace with God.

   If God has declared you righteous in His Son, no accusation has authority to remove you.

Prayer

Father,

We thank You for the gospel of God, promised in the Scriptures and fulfilled in Your Son, Jesus Christ our Lord. By Your Spirit, grant us eyes to see Christ as the only Door, hearts to trust Him fully, and lives ordered by obedience of faith. Establish us in grace, surround us with peace, and keep us from building our confidence on anything less than Your finished work. We pray to You,

In the name of Jesus Christ. Amen.

Fortress of Justification

2

The Inner Approach

First, I thank my God through Jesus Christ for you all, that your faith is spoken of throughout the whole world.

For God is my witness, whom I serve with my spirit in the gospel of his Son, that without ceasing I make mention of you always in my prayers;

Making request, if by any means now at length I might have a prosperous journey by the will of God to come unto you.

For I long to see you, that I may impart unto you some spiritual gift, to the end ye may be established;

That is, that I may be comforted together with you by the mutual faith both of you and me.

Now I would not have you ignorant, brethren, that oftentimes I purposed to come unto you, (but was let hitherto,) that I might have some fruit among you also, even as among other Gentiles.

I am debtor both to the Greeks, and to the Barbarians; both to the wise, and to the unwise.

So, as much as in me is, I am ready to preach the gospel to you that are at Rome also. (Romans 1:8–15)

Once a traveler has passed through the gate of a fortress, there is often a stretch of protected ground before the central keep is reached. It is a place of orientation—where one learns the purpose of the stronghold, the character of its builders, and the reason it exists at all.

Romans 1:8–15 occupies that space.

Here Paul reveals his heart toward the Roman believers, his obligation to the world, and his eagerness to preach the gospel in the very center of imperial power. Before he proclaims the righteousness of God, he establishes the pastoral and missionary urgency that drives everything he is about to say.

A Thankful Apostle

"First, I thank my God through Jesus Christ for you all, that your faith is spoken of throughout the whole world." (Romans 1:8)

Paul begins not with correction, but with gratitude.

The Roman church is known for its faith, not for its perfection. That distinction matters. Faith here does not mean flawless theology or harmony without tension. It means a genuine trust in Christ that has endured public visibility in a city where allegiance to anyone other than Caesar was viewed with suspicion.

Paul thanks his God through Jesus Christ, reminding the reader that even gratitude is mediated through Christ. God is approached, thanked, and praised only on the ground Christ has provided.

The faith of the Romans is "spoken of throughout the whole world"—not because Rome is spiritually superior, but because Rome is visible. Faith lived out in the capital inevitably becomes known. This visibility raises the stakes: a divided church in Rome will echo division outward; a justified church will echo stability.

A Praying Servant

"For God is my witness, whom I serve with my spirit in the gospel of his Son, that without ceasing I make mention of you always in my prayers;

Making request, if by any means now at length I might have a prosperous journey by the will of God to come unto you." (Romans 1:9–10)

Paul reinforces his sincerity by appealing to God as witness. His concern for Rome is not strategic flattery; it is spiritual labor.

He describes his service as something done "with my spirit"—not mechanically, not professionally, but inwardly. The gospel is not a role Paul performs; it is a calling that engages his whole being.

His prayers reveal two truths held together:

• Persistent intercession: *"without ceasing."*

• Submission to God's will: *"by the will of God."*

Paul longs to come to Rome, but he refuses to demand it. Even apostolic ambition bows to divine providence. The fortress Paul builds rests on God's timing, not human control.

A Desire to Establish, Not Impress

"For I long to see you, that I may impart unto you some spiritual gift, to the end ye may be established;

That is, that I may be comforted together with you by the mutual faith both of you and me."
(Romans 1:11–12)

Paul's purpose in visiting Rome is not dominance or display. He does not intend to overwhelm the church with apostolic authority or to showcase theological brilliance. His aim is establishment—to strengthen, stabilize, and root them firmly.

Yet Paul immediately guards against misunderstanding. He clarifies that this strengthening is mutual. The apostle expects to be encouraged by their faith just as they are encouraged by his. This mutuality undermines every hierarchy Rome's culture instinctively promotes.

In the fortress of the gospel, even apostles stand alongside ordinary believers as fellow recipients of grace.

A Delayed Visit, Not a Disregarded Church

"Now I would not have you ignorant, brethren, that oftentimes I purposed to come unto you, (but was let hitherto,) that I might have some fruit among you also, even as among other Gentiles." (Romans 1:13)

Paul anticipates suspicion. Why has he not come sooner? Why has Rome not received apostolic attention directly?

The answer is not reluctance, but restraint. Paul has been hindered—by circumstance, calling, and providence. His desire has always been to see fruit in Rome as he has elsewhere.

This matters pastorally. Distance can easily be interpreted as disinterest. Paul ensures the Roman believers know that his absence is not neglect.

A Debt to the World

"I am debtor both to the Greeks, and to the Barbarians; both to the wise, and to the unwise." (Romans 1:14)

Here Paul names the driving force behind his mission: obligation.

He calls himself a debtor, not because the world deserves the gospel, but because God has entrusted him with it. To possess good news is to owe its proclamation.

Paul deliberately erases social distinctions:

• Greek and Barbarian (cultured and uncultured),

• Wise and unwise (educated and uneducated).

The gospel does not recognize Rome's hierarchy. Every category that determines worth in the empire collapses before the universal need for salvation.

Ready to Preach in Rome

"So, as much as in me is, I am ready to preach the gospel to you that are at Rome also." *(Romans 1:15)*

Paul ends this section with resolve.

Rome is the seat of power, culture, and intimidation. Philosophers debate there. Emperors rule there. Armies march at its command. Yet Paul declares himself ready—eager, willing, prepared—to preach the same gospel there that he has preached everywhere else.

This statement prepares the way for what follows. If Paul is ready to preach in Rome, the reason must be more than confidence in his rhetoric. And so he will immediately explain why:

"For I am not ashamed of the gospel of Christ:"
(Romans 1:16)

Summary

Romans 1:8–15 reveals the heart behind the doctrine.

Paul thanks God for the Roman believers, prays for them continually, longs to strengthen them, and views himself as indebted to the entire world. His eagerness to preach in Rome is not ambition, but obedience. Before explaining justification, Paul demonstrates the humility, urgency, and universality of the gospel that makes justification necessary.

The inner approach leads directly to the drawbridge.

Application

1. Give thanks for faith before correcting weakness.

    Paul models gratitude even toward a divided church.

2. Submit godly desire to God's will.

    Longing without surrender leads to frustration; surrender leads to trust.

3. Seek establishment, not recognition.

   Spiritual maturity aims at stability, not status.

4. Live as a debtor, not a consumer.

   The gospel entrusted to us obligates us to others.

5. Be ready to speak Christ wherever God places you.

   No city, culture, or power structure diminishes the gospel's authority.

Prayer

Father,

We thank You for the faith You have kindled among Your people. Teach us to pray without ceasing, to submit our plans to Your will, and to seek the strengthening of one another rather than our own prominence. Make us faithful stewards of the gospel entrusted to us, ready to proclaim Christ wherever You have placed us. Establish us in grace and prepare our hearts for the truth yet to come. We pray to You,

In the name of Jesus Christ. Amen.

Fortress of Justification

3

The

Drawbridge
of Faith

For I am not ashamed of the gospel of Christ: for it is the power of God unto salvation to every one that believeth; to the Jew first, and also to the Greek.

For therein is the righteousness of God revealed from faith to faith: as it is written, The just shall live by faith.(Romans 1:16–17)

Every fortress has a decisive crossing point—a place where the traveler can no longer rely on familiar ground. Romans 1:16–17 is that crossing. It is not an aside, a clarification, or an apology. It is the thesis statement of the Epistle to the

Romans and the interpretive key to everything that follows.

Paul is not excusing himself for preaching something elementary. He is declaring that the gospel of Christ is the driving force of the entire Christian life and the full revelation of the righteousness of God.

Not an Apology, but a Thesis

"For I am not ashamed of the gospel of Christ..." (Romans 1:16a)

This statement is often misunderstood. Paul is not embarrassed by the gospel, nor does he fear that the Romans will consider it beneath them. The word translated *ashamed* carries the sense of hesitation, stumbling, or being tripped up. Paul is rejecting the notion that the gospel is an obstacle—something to move past on the way to deeper truths.

In Rome, both Jews and Gentiles had reasons to stumble.

Jews could trip over a righteousness that did not center on the law.

Gentiles could trip over a salvation that did not rest on wisdom, power, or status.

Paul confronts both instincts at once. The gospel is not the starting block to be left behind. It is the path itself.

The Gospel as the Ongoing Power of God

"...for it is the power of God unto salvation to every one that believeth..." (Romans 1:16b)

Paul explains why the gospel cannot be outgrown: it is the power of God unto salvation.

The Greek word δύναμις (*dynamis*) is often associated with dynamite, but that image is misleading. Dynamite acts once, produces immediate change, and is spent. Paul is not describing a momentary explosion that initiates salvation and then fades.

A far more fitting image—also rooted in *dynamis*—is a **dynamo**: a source that continually generates power.

Paul is not speaking only of the instant of conversion. He is speaking of salvation as a whole—begun, sustained, and completed by the gospel. The death, burial, and resurrection of Jesus Christ do not merely open the door to salvation; they power the entire redemptive life.

The gospel is the dynamo that drives:

- redemption and propitiation,

- regeneration and justification,

- sanctification and endurance,

- guidance and obedience,

- and ultimately resurrection.

To disconnect from the gospel after conversion is not maturity. It is spiritual collapse. The gospel does not hand us off to law, technique, or self-mastery. It carries us from first faith to final glory.

Faith as the Means of Connection

"...to every one that believeth..." (Romans 1:16c)

Power must be received.

A dynamo may run continuously, but unless something is connected to it, nothing is illuminated. Faith is not the source of salvation; faith is the connection to the source. It does not generate power—it receives it.

This is true for everyone, without distinction. Faith, not heritage or achievement, is the means by which the gospel's power is experienced.

One Gospel, One Righteous God

"...to the Jew first, and also to the Greek."
(Romans 1:16d)

This phrase establishes history, not hierarchy. The gospel was announced first within Israel's story—through covenant, law, and promise—but it was never confined there. What was entrusted to Israel was always intended for the nations.

Paul dismantles every claim to advantage. There is not one gospel for Jews and another for Gentiles. There is one gospel because there is one righteous God.

The Righteousness Revealed Is God's Own

"For therein is the righteousness of God revealed..." (Romans 1:17a)

Here Paul identifies the deepest significance of the gospel.

He does not say that the gospel reveals the righteousness given to believers—though that truth will follow. He says that the gospel reveals *the righteousness of God*. This is not primarily about our moral standing, but about God's character.

The gospel reveals that God has not laid aside His justice to show mercy, nor restrained His mercy to preserve justice. Instead, God has satisfied both in the work of His Son.

- God's righteousness is revealed in His wrath against sin.

- God's righteousness is revealed in His refusal to ignore evil.

- God's righteousness is revealed in His provision of propitiation and atonement.

- God's righteousness is revealed in His faithfulness to His promises.

- God's righteousness is revealed in His ability to justify sinners without compromising holiness.

The gospel does not soften God. It vindicates Him.

From Faith to Faith

"...from faith to faith..." (Romans 1:17b)

This phrase describes the manner in which God's righteousness is revealed and received. It is not achieved by effort or perceived by intellect. It is known by faith from beginning to end.

God's righteous character is displayed in the gospel, and faith recognizes, trusts, and rests in that righteousness—at conversion, throughout life, and unto resurrection.

Faith does not improve God's righteousness. It lives in confidence that God is righteous.

The Life That Righteousness Sustains

"...as it is written, The just shall live by faith."
(Romans 1:17c)

Paul anchors his thesis in Habakkuk, where the issue is not personal guilt alone but trust in God's righteous actions amid judgment and confusion.

The righteous live by faith because God's righteousness is trustworthy—even when His ways are severe, even when His judgments are heavy, and even when His mercy seems astonishing.

This is why Romans will begin with wrath and end with unity. The same righteousness governs both.

Summary

Romans 1:16–17 is the thesis of the Epistle.

Paul declares that the gospel of Christ is the ongoing power of God that carries salvation from beginning to end. In that gospel, God reveals not a diminished righteousness, but His own perfect character— righteous in wrath, righteous in mercy, righteous in redemption, and righteous in reconciliation. Faith is the means by which this righteousness is trusted, and life itself is sustained by continued dependence on the gospel.

The drawbridge is not crossed once and forgotten. It is the only way forward.

Application

1. Do not treat the gospel as a past event.

   If the gospel is not powering your present life, something else is.

2. Trust God's righteousness, not your under-standing.

   Faith rests in who God is, not merely in what He gives.

3. Refuse every attempt to soften or segment God's character.

   The God who judges sin is the same God who saves sinners.

4. Live connected.

The righteous do not outgrow faith; they live by it.

Prayer

Father,

We praise You for the gospel of Your Son, Jesus Christ, in which Your righteousness is fully revealed. Keep us from stumbling over grace or doubting Your justice. Teach us to trust You wholly—to live by faith from beginning to end—drawing all our life, strength, and hope from the gospel You have provided. Establish us in Your righteousness, and carry us safely to the day of resurrection. We pray to You,

In the name of Jesus Christ. Amen.

Fortress of Justification

4

The Good News That God is Angry

For the wrath of God is revealed from heaven against all ungodliness and unrighteousness of men, who hold the truth in unrighteousness;

Because that which may be known of God is manifest in them; for God hath shewed it unto them.

For the invisible things of him from the creation of the world are clearly seen, being understood by the things that are made, even his eternal power and Godhead; so that they are without excuse:

35

Because that, when they knew God, they glorified him not as God, neither were thankful; but became vain in their imaginations, and their foolish heart was darkened.

Professing themselves to be wise, they became fools,

And changed the glory of the uncorruptible God into an image made like to corruptible man, and to birds, and fourfooted beasts, and creeping things.

Wherefore God also gave them up to uncleanness through the lusts of their own hearts, to dishonour their own bodies between themselves:

Who changed the truth of God into a lie, and worshipped and served the creature more than the Creator, who is blessed for ever. Amen.

For this cause God gave them up unto vile affections: for even their women did change the natural use into that which is against nature:

And likewise also the men, leaving the natural use of the woman, burned in their lust one toward another; men with men working that which is unseemly, and receiving in themselves that recompence of their error which was meet.

And even as they did not like to retain God in their knowledge, God gave them over to a reprobate mind, to do those things which are not convenient;

Being filled with all unrighteousness, fornication, wickedness, covetousness, maliciousness; full of envy, murder, debate, deceit, malignity; whisperers,

Backbiters, haters of God, despiteful, proud, boasters, inventors of evil things, disobedient to parents,

Without understanding, covenantbreakers, without natural affection, implacable, unmerciful:

Who knowing the judgment of God, that they which commit such things are worthy of death, not only do the same, but have pleasure in them that do them. (Romans 1:18-32) f Romans 1:16–17 is the drawbridge into the fortress, Romans 1:18–32 is the chasm the drawbridge must cross. Paul has just declared that the gospel reveals the righteousness of God. Now he begins to show what that means in the first and most unsettling way: God's righteousness is revealed in His wrath.

That is why this passage feels frightening. It is meant to.

But Paul is not changing the subject. He is proving his thesis. If the gospel truly reveals God's righteousness, then the gospel must first tell the truth about God's holy anger against sin. A God who could tolerate sin would not be righteous. A God who could shrug at evil would not be good. The good news begins here—not because wrath is pleasant, but because righteousness is necessary.

Wrath Revealed "From Heaven"

"For the wrath of God is revealed from heaven against all ungodliness and unrighteousness of men, who hold the truth in unrighteousness;" (Romans 1:18)

Paul's first word is *"for"*—because this explains why the gospel is necessary and why God's righteousness matters.

The wrath of God is revealed from heaven. It is not an earthly mood or a human projection. It is not the tantrum of a deity whose pride has been wounded. It is the settled, holy response of the righteous God who reigns from a place of perfect purity.

And notice its scope: it is against *all* ungodliness and unrighteousness.

- Unrighteousness is doing what is wrong.

- Ungodliness is more basic: living as though God is not there.

Paul lists ungodliness first because the root of human sin is not merely bad actions. It is the refusal of God Himself. We live in His world, under His providence, breathing His air, receiving His gifts—and we carry on as though we owe Him nothing.

This is not only the sin of criminals. It is the quiet rebellion of ordinary life lived without worship.

God's Wrath Is Righteous Because We Suppress Known Truth

Paul says that men "hold" the truth in unrighteousness —better understood as suppressing the truth. The problem is not ignorance; it is resistance. The image is not of a student who lacks information, but of a guard who restrains a prisoner. Truth presses upward with moral force, but fallen humanity applies pressure in the opposite direction. Like a beach ball forced beneath the surface of the water, the truth must be actively pushed down, for left alone it will rise. This suppression requires effort, not apathy. Men do not stumble into unbelief; they labor to keep God's revelation from disrupting their autonomy. What condemns humanity, therefore, is not the absence of light, but the deliberate refusal to let that light shine where it would demand repentance, obedience, and worship.

> *"Because that which may be known of God is manifest in them; for God hath shewed it unto them." (Romans 1:19)*

There is truth about God that is "manifest"—plainly shown. God is not hiding while judging. He is revealing while humanity is resisting.

> *"For the invisible things of him from the creation of the world are clearly seen, being understood by the things that are made, even his eternal power and Godhead; so that they are without excuse:" (Romans 1:20)*

Creation is not salvation, but creation is testimony. It does not tell us everything, but it tells us enough to remove the excuse of "I did not know." The ordered world bears witness to an ordered Maker. The vastness and interdependence of creation testify to

"His eternal power." The reality of moral structure and meaning points to "Godhead."

So God's wrath is not arbitrary. It is righteous because it comes against those who resist what God has made plain.

The First Step Downward: Ingratitude

"Because that, when they knew God, they glorified him not as God, neither were thankful..." (Romans 1:21)

Paul describes the beginning of collapse with two failures:

• They did not glorify Him as God.

• They were not thankful.

This is where ungodliness becomes visible. A person may appear outwardly decent, yet live with a heart that does not worship and does not thank. Such a life is not neutral. It is rebellious.

When gratitude dies, worship dies. And when worship dies, the mind does not remain clear:

"...but became vain in their imaginations, and their foolish heart was darkened." (Romans 1:21)

The Great Exchange: Glory for Images

"Professing themselves to be wise, they became fools,"

"And changed the glory of the uncorruptible God into an image..." (Romans 1:22–23)

Here is the irony: humanity claims wisdom while committing the most irrational act of all—exchanging the glory of the incorruptible God for something corruptible.

This exchange does not always begin with statues. It begins whenever the creature refuses the Creator's weight. People prefer gods they can manage—gods that do not judge, gods that do not command, gods that do not demand repentance: a "higher power" of our own choosing.

And this is why idolatry is not merely "ancient religion." It is the perennial human strategy for escaping the righteousness of God.

The Wrath That Looks Like "Giving Over"

This is one of the most sobering parts of the chapter. God's wrath is revealed not only in future judgment, but in present abandonment.

> *"Wherefore God also gave them up to uncleanness through the lusts of their own hearts..." (Romans 1:24)*

The phrase "gave them up" (or "gave them over") appears as a refrain. Paul is describing a form of judgment that does not always arrive as fire from heaven. **It arrives as God letting sinners have what they insist upon.**

God's commands are not arbitrary restrictions; they are warnings—signposts that protect life. When men refuse God's right to rule, God's wrath may be revealed in this terrifying sentence: *Very well—have it your way.*

Paul then includes sexual rebellion as a prominent example of what this abandonment looks like in the body and in desire. He is not isolating one sin as though it were the only sin that matters. He is showing what happens when the creature refuses the Creator: disorder spreads inward and outward.

The Deepening Judgment: A Reprobate Mind

"And even as they did not like to retain God in their knowledge, God gave them over to a reprobate mind, to do those things which are not convenient;" (Romans 1:28)

This is not merely moral weakness; it is moral distortion. A "reprobate mind" is a mind that no longer functions properly. It becomes bent. It justifies what should shame it. It celebrates what should grieve it. It condemns righteousness and defends corruption.

The judgment fits the crime: they did not want God in their knowledge—so God gives them over to the consequences of thinking without God.

The Catalogue That Levels Us All

Paul now lists a sweeping portrait of human evil:

"Being filled with all unrighteousness, fornication, wickedness, covetousness, maliciousness..."

"Full of envy, murder, debate, deceit, malignity..."

"Whisperers, backbiters, haters of God, despiteful, proud, boasters..."

"Disobedient to parents..."

"Without understanding... covenantbreakers... without natural affection... implacable... unmerciful..." (Romans 1:29–31)

This is where Paul prevents the reader from using Romans 1 as a telescope to inspect everyone else.

Yes, the passage includes the sins that society likes to spotlight. But it also includes the sins we like to excuse—pride, gossip, slander, envy, disobedience, lack of understanding, coldness of heart.

Paul does not allow a righteous spectator. He brings every man into the dock.

The Final Darkness: Approval

"Who knowing the judgment of God, that they which commit such things are worthy of death, not only do the same, but have pleasure in them that do them." (Romans 1:32)

The final step is not merely sin—it is celebration of sin. It is the moral inversion where the conscience no longer warns but applauds.

This is why the good news must be more than advice. We do not need minor improvement. We need rescue.

And here is where the chapter earns its title:

The good news is that God is angry.

If God were not angry at sin, then sin would be eternal. Oppression would be permanent. Violence would be tolerated. Corruption would be normal. The universe would be morally unstable, and God would be unworthy of worship.

But the gospel announces a righteous God who does not tolerate sin—and then, astonishingly, provides a way to save sinners without compromising His righteousness.

Romans begins with wrath, but it does not end with wrath. The same righteousness that reveals God's anger will reveal God's provision—propitiation, atonement, justification, and a reconciled people made one in Christ.

Summary

Romans 1:18–32 demonstrates the first great revelation of God's righteousness: His wrath against sin. Humanity is not condemned for lack of light, but for suppressing known truth. The downward spiral begins with refusal to glorify and thank God, moves into idolatrous exchange, and culminates in God "giving over" sinners to the consequences of their rebellion—desires, disorder, and a reprobate mind. The passage closes with the darkest note: not only sin, but approval of sin.

The good news is not that God ignores evil. The good news is that God is righteous—and therefore He will deal with sin truly, fully, and finally.

Application

1. Stop treating ungodliness as harmless.

   Living as though God is not there is not neutrality —it is rebellion.

2. Let Romans 1 accuse you before it instructs you.

   This chapter was not written to arm us against "their" sins, but to expose our hearts.

3. Fear the judgment of being "given over."

   One of the most terrifying forms of wrath is God allowing a man to harden himself comfortably.

4. Recover gratitude as a spiritual safeguard.

   Ingratitude is not a small flaw; it is often the first step into darkness.

5. Run to Christ, not to comparison.

The point of this passage is not moral superiority but desperate need of a Savior.

Prayer

Father,

We tremble before Your righteousness. You are holy, and Your wrath against sin is just. Deliver us from the blindness of ungodliness, from the pride that compares itself to others, and from the folly that suppresses the truth. Grant us repentance where we have grown cold, gratitude where we have been entitled, and fear where we have been careless. And we thank You that Your gospel does not end with wrath, but reveals Your perfect provision in Jesus Christ. Draw our hearts to Your Son, and keep us in the refuge You have built. We pray to You,

In the name of Jesus Christ. Amen.

5

Still on the Road

Therefore thou art inexcusable, O man, whosoever thou art that judgest: for wherein thou judgest another, thou condemnest thyself; for thou that judgest doest the same things.

But we are sure that the judgment of God is according to truth against them which commit such things.

And thinkest thou this, O man, that judgest them which do such things, and doest the same, that thou shalt escape the judgment of God?

49

Or despisest thou the riches of his goodness and forbearance and longsuffering; not knowing that the goodness of God leadeth thee to repentance?

But after thy hardness and impenitent heart treasurest up unto thyself wrath against the day of wrath and revelation of the righteous judgment of God;

Who will render to every man according to his deeds:

To them who by patient continuance in well doing seek for glory and honour and immortality, eternal life:

But unto them that are contentious, and do not obey the truth, but obey unrighteousness, indignation and wrath,

Tribulation and anguish, upon every soul of man that doeth evil, of the Jew first, and also of the Gentile;

But glory, honour, and peace, to every man that worketh good, to the Jew first, and also to the Gentile:

For there is no respect of persons with God.

For as many as have sinned without law shall also perish without law: and as many as have sinned in the law shall be judged by the law;

(For not the hearers of the law are just before God, but the doers of the law shall be justified.

For when the Gentiles, which have not the law, do by nature the things contained in the law, these, having not the law, are a law unto themselves:

Which shew the work of the law written in their hearts, their conscience also bearing witness, and their thoughts the mean while accusing or else excusing one another;)

In the day when God shall judge the secrets of men by Jesus Christ according to my gospel. (Romans 2:1-16)

After Romans 1, no honest reader should feel comfortable. The landscape Paul has described is barren, chaotic, and dangerous. Humanity is not wandering aimlessly; it is traveling steadily toward a precipice—the day of wrath and the revelation of the righteous judgment of God.

But there is a familiar human instinct that emerges in dangerous places: comparison.

Romans 2 addresses the man who, having heard the catalogue of sins in Romans 1, breathes a quiet sigh of relief and says, "At least I am not like them." He is still on the same road, under the same sky, moving toward the same cliff—but he believes himself safer because he is not driving as recklessly.

Paul dismantles that illusion.

The Inexcusable Man

"Therefore thou art inexcusable, O man, whosoever thou art that judgest: for wherein thou judgest another, thou condemnest thyself; for thou that judgest doest the same things." *(Romans 2:1)*

The word *therefore* connects Romans 2 directly to Romans 1. Paul has not changed subjects. He has turned his attention.

The man addressed here is not irreligious. He is not indifferent. He is morally alert. He recognizes evil when he sees it—and that recognition is precisely the problem.

Paul does not say this man should stop judging. Judgment is inevitable. Everyone judges. The issue is not whether he judges, but what his judgment proves. When he condemns another, he admits that right and wrong exist. He confesses a standard. And in doing so, he condemns himself—not because he commits the same sins in identical form, but because he belongs to the same category: a creature who knows what is right and does not live up to it.

The judging man is not standing above the road. He is still on it. His moral clarity does not remove him from danger; it testifies that he knows better.

That is why Paul calls him inexcusable. Ignorance is no refuge. His own verdicts have already testified against him.

Judgment According to Truth

"But we are sure that the judgment of God is according to truth against them which commit such things." (Romans 2:2–3)

Human judgment is selective. God's judgment is true.

It is not based on reputation or comparison. It is not softened by sincerity or intention. It does not overlook private sins because public ones are absent. God judges according to what is—not what appears to be.

"And thinkest thou this, O man... that thou shalt escape the judgment of God?" (Romans 2:3)

This is the road illusion in its purest form: "Yes, judgment is real—but it is for others." Paul exposes the absurdity of that hope. The man who recognizes judgment but assumes exemption is not discerning; he is deceived.

Delayed judgment is not denied judgment. The road still ends where it ends.

Kindness Mistaken for Safety

"Or despisest thou the riches of his goodness and forbearance and longsuffering; not knowing that the goodness of God leadeth thee to repentance?" (Romans 2:4)

God is good. He is patient. He restrains immediate judgment. And men misread that patience as indifference.

Paul says this is not mere misunderstanding—it is contempt. To treat God's patience as permission is to despise it. His goodness is not an endorsement of the road; it is an invitation to leave it.

The delay of judgment is mercy, not safety. It is time given to turn around—not proof that the cliff is imaginary.

Treasuring Up Wrath

"But after thy hardness and impenitent heart treasurest up unto thyself wrath against the day of wrath and revelation of the righteous judgment of God." (Romans 2:5)

This is one of the most terrifying descriptions in Scripture.

God is not becoming progressively angrier. The sinner is becoming progressively fixed. Hardness is not emotion; it is will. An impenitent heart is not merely unfeeling—it is *unturning.*

Paul describes a man who continues forward, ignoring warnings, refusing exits, mistaking motion for progress. Every mile traveled adds momentum. Every refusal to turn increases the force of the eventual collision.

Wrath is not stored in God's temperament; it is stored in the sinner's trajectory.

The road does not bend. The cliff does not retreat. The longer one travels, the less able one is to stop.

Impartial Judgment

"Who will render to every man according to his deeds." (Romans 2:6–11)

Paul states a principle that dismantles every refuge of privilege: God judges impartially. Ethnicity does not alter the destination. Religious identity does not change the terrain.

"To the Jew first, and also to the Gentile" is not advantage—it is accountability. Greater light brings greater responsibility. But the outcome is the same: God renders to each according to deeds.

Paul is not yet explaining how anyone is saved. He is establishing that no one escapes by category. If judgment is according to deeds, then labels cannot save. Moral comparison cannot save. Possession of truth cannot save.

The road claims everyone who stays on it.

The Law Written Within

"For as many as have sinned without law shall also perish without law..." (Romans 2:12–15)

Ignorance does not rescue the Gentile. Possession does not rescue the Jew. Why? Because God has left no one without witness.

Even those without the written law show "the work of the law written in their hearts." Conscience testifies. Thoughts accuse and excuse. The inner courtroom never adjourns.

Conscience does not justify—but it condemns. It proves that humanity is not lost in darkness, but resisting light.

Judgment of Secrets

"In the day when God shall judge the secrets of men by Jesus Christ according to my gospel." (Romans 2:16)

Paul ends this section where he must: at judgment.

Not public judgment only. Not cultural judgment. Judgment of secrets. Hidden motives. Private rationalizations. Unseen compromises.

And the Judge is Jesus Christ.

Here, Christ is not yet presented as refuge—but as authority. The One who will later justify sinners will first expose them. No one on the road escapes His gaze.

Summary

Romans 2 exposes the false safety of moral comparison. The judging man is not above judgment; he is condemned by the standard he affirms. God's patience is not approval, but mercy meant to lead to repentance. Hardness and impenitence do not delay wrath—they store it up. God judges impartially, whether Jew or Gentile, with or without the written law, according to truth. Conscience itself bears witness, and even hidden things will be revealed when God judges the secrets of men by Jesus Christ.

The road remains the same.

The cliff remains ahead.

And no one escapes by claiming to drive better.

Application

1. Stop mistaking comparison for safety.

    Being less visible, less scandalous, or less offensive does not remove you from judgment.

2. Treat God's patience as an invitation, not a cushion.

    Mercy delays judgment so you may turn—not so you may continue comfortably.

3. Fear hardness more than guilt.

    A heart that can still repent is alive. A heart that will not turn is in mortal danger.

4. Listen to what your judgments reveal about you.

    If you know right from wrong, you know enough to be accountable.

5. Do not assume the road ends gently.

    The cliff is real. The delay is mercy. The call is to turn—while turning is still possible.

Prayer

Father,

We confess that we have judged others while excusing ourselves, mistaking Your patience for safety and Your kindness for approval. Expose the hardness of our wills and deliver us from the deception of delay. Grant us repentance while the road still allows turning, and awaken us to the danger of continuing comfortably toward judgment. Keep us from trusting comparison, excuse, or familiarity with truth. Teach us to fear rightly, that we may yet seek refuge where You have provided it.

We pray to You,

In the name of Jesus Christ. Amen.

6

Still on the Road — With the Map in Hand

Behold, thou art called a Jew, and restest in the law, and makest thy boast of God,

And knowest his will, and approvest the things that are more excellent, being instructed out of the law;

And art confident that thou thyself art a guide of the blind, a light of them which are in darkness,

An instructor of the foolish, a teacher of babes, which hast the form of knowledge and of the truth in the law.

Thou therefore which teachest another, teachest thou not thyself? thou that preachest a man should not steal, dost thou steal?

Thou that sayest a man should not commit adultery, dost thou commit adultery? thou that abhorrest idols, dost thou commit sacrilege?

Thou that makest thy boast of the law, through breaking the law dishonourest thou God?

For the name of God is blasphemed among the Gentiles through you, as it is written.

For circumcision verily profiteth, if thou keep the law: but if thou be a breaker of the law, thy circumcision is made uncircumcision.

Therefore if the uncircumcision keep the righteousness of the law, shall not his uncircumcision be counted for circumcision?

And shall not uncircumcision which is by nature, if it fulfil the law, judge thee, who by the letter and circumcision dost transgress the law?

For he is not a Jew, which is one outwardly; neither is that circumcision, which is outward in the flesh:

But he is a Jew, which is one inwardly; and circumcision is that of the heart, in the spirit, and not in the letter; whose praise is not of men, but of God. (Romans 2:17-29)

Romans 2 has already dismantled one illusion of safety: moral comparison. The man who condemns others is not safer than the openly corrupt; he is merely more articulate about standards he does not keep.

But Paul knows there is a second, more fortified illusion still standing—one that feels far sturdier than moral intuition. It is not merely judgment that now claims security, but religion.

Romans 2:17–29 addresses the man who is still on the road, still moving toward judgment, but who believes himself safe because he knows God's law, bears God's covenant mark, and identifies himself with God's people. He is not guessing about right and wrong; he possesses Scripture. And that possession, he believes, must count for something.

Paul will show that it counts—for accountability.

Confidence Built on Possession

"Behold, thou art called a Jew, and restest in the law, and makest thy boast of God..." (Romans 2:17–20)

Paul now names the man directly. This is not the pagan outsider. This is the insider. He carries the right name, rests in the law, boasts in God, knows His will, and approves what is excellent because he has been instructed from the Scriptures.

This man is confident. Confident enough to see himself as:

• a guide to the blind,

• a light to those in darkness,

• an instructor of the foolish,

• a teacher of children.

None of this is false. The tragedy is not that he knows the truth, but that he believes knowing it places him above judgment.

He is still on the same road—but now he holds the map and assumes that possession equals safety.

The Question Religion Cannot Answer

"Thou therefore which teachest another, teachest thou not thyself?" (Romans 2:21)

Paul does not challenge the law. He applies it.He does not ask whether the man teaches truth. He asks whether the man lives under it.

Thou therefore which teachest another, teachest thou not thyself? thou that preachest a man should not steal, dost thou steal?

Thou that sayest a man should not commit adultery, dost thou commit adultery? thou that abhorrest idols, dost thou commit sacrilege?

Thou that makest thy boast of the law, through breaking the law dishonourest thou God? (Romans 2:21-23)

Paul's point is not hypocrisy in isolated acts; it is contradiction at the level of identity. The law condemns not only flagrant rebellion, but selective obedience.

And the result is devastating—not only personally, but publicly:

"For the name of God is blasphemed among the Gentiles through you," (Romans 2:24)

The religious man believes he honors God by possessing the law. Paul says he dishonors God by breaking it. Knowledge without obedience does not glorify God—it defames Him.

The road is not safer because Scripture is quoted on it.

Covenant Marks Without Covenant Faithfulness

"For circumcision verily profiteth, if thou keep the law: but if thou be a breaker of the law, thy circumcision is made uncircumcision." *(Romans 2:25–27)*

Paul now touches the most sensitive point of all: covenant identity.

Circumcision mattered. It was given by God. It marked belonging to the covenant people. But Paul makes a claim that would have sounded unthinkable: the mark means nothing if the covenant is broken.

The sign was never meant to replace obedience; it was meant to testify to it. When the law is broken, the sign does not protect—it indicts.

And Paul presses the logic further. If an uncircumcised man keeps the righteous requirements of the law, will he not condemn the circumcised lawbreaker?

The shock is intentional. Possession of privilege does not reverse judgment. In fact, it intensifies it.

The road does not change because one belongs to a historic people. The cliff does not move because one carries a badge.

The Redefinition of Identity

"For he is not a Jew, which is one outwardly...

But he is a Jew, which is one inwardly; and circumcision is that of the heart, in the spirit, and not in the letter..." (Romans 2:28–29)

Here Paul quietly dismantles the final refuge of religious confidence: external identity.

True covenant belonging is not defined by flesh, ritual, or heritage. It is defined by inward reality. Not by letter, but by spirit. Not by public approval, but by divine recognition.

"Whose praise is not of men, but of God." *(Romans 2:29)*

This is not yet the gospel. Paul has not explained how such a heart is created. He has only established that no outward marker can produce it.

The religious man is still on the road—but now he has lost the comfort of thinking he belongs somewhere else.

Summary

Romans 2:17–29 exposes the false refuge of religious identity. Possessing the law does not excuse breaking it. Teaching truth does not replace obedience. Covenant signs without covenant faithfulness offer no protection. External marks cannot substitute for inward reality. The Jew who rests in the law and boasts in God stands under the same judgment as the Gentile—because God judges not by possession, but by truth. Identity without obedience does not remove one from the road; it only deepens accountability.

Application

1. Do not confuse proximity to truth with protection from judgment.

   Knowing God's word does not neutralize its demands.

2. Let Scripture judge you before you use it to instruct others.

   The law is a mirror before it is a megaphone.

3. Fear outward religion that lacks inward obedience.

   Covenant signs cannot rescue a covenant breaker.

4. Refuse identity built on heritage, ritual, or reputation.

   God's judgment penetrates beyond labels to the heart.

5. Do not mistake belonging for obedience.

   The road does not change because you know where it ends.

Prayer

Father,

We confess how easily we rest in knowledge while resisting obedience, how quickly we boast in truth we do not live. Strip us of every false confidence built on possession, heritage, or outward form. Expose the ways we have used Your law to judge others while excusing ourselves. Deliver us from religious security that leaves the heart unchanged. Grant us eyes to see that outward marks cannot save, and awaken us to our true condition before You.

We pray to You,

In the name of Jesus Christ. Amen.

7

The End of the Road

What advantage then hath the Jew? or what profit is there of circumcision?

Much every way: chiefly, because that unto them were committed the oracles of God.

For what if some did not believe? shall their unbelief make the faith of God without effect?

God forbid: yea, let God be true, but every man a liar; as it is written, That thou mightest be justified in thy sayings, and mightest overcome when thou art judged.

But if our unrighteousness commend the righteousness of God, what shall we say? Is God unrighteous who taketh vengeance? (I speak as a man)

God forbid: for then how shall God judge the world?

For if the truth of God hath more abounded through my lie unto his glory; why yet am I also judged as a sinner?

And not rather, (as we be slanderously reported, and as some affirm that we say,) Let us do evil, that good may come? whose damnation is just.

What then? are we better than they? No, in no wise: for we have before proved both Jews and Gentiles, that they are all under sin;

As it is written, There is none righteous, no, not one:

There is none that understandeth, there is none that seeketh after God.

They are all gone out of the way, they are together become unprofitable; there is none that doeth good, no, not one.

Their throat is an open sepulchre; with their tongues they have used deceit; the poison of asps is under their lips:

Whose mouth is full of cursing and bitterness:

Their feet are swift to shed blood:

Destruction and misery are in their ways:

And the way of peace have they not known:

There is no fear of God before their eyes.

Now we know that what things soever the law saith, it saith to them who are under the law: that every mouth may be stopped, and all the world may become guilty before God.

Therefore by the deeds of the law there shall no flesh be justified in his sight: for by the law is the knowledge of sin. (Romans 3:1-20)

Up to this point, Paul has removed every false confidence without yet offering escape. In Romans 1, the road's destination was exposed: wrath revealed against ungodliness. In Romans 2:1–16, the moral man learned that judgment applies to him as well. In Romans 2:17–29, the religious man discovered that possessing the law does not protect him from it.

Now Paul reaches the unavoidable conclusion.

Romans 3:1–20 is not a new argument. It is the verdict. The road does not continue. There is no alternate route. There is no safe shoulder to pull onto. Humanity has reached the edge—and there is nowhere left to stand.

The Question That Cannot Save

"What advantage then hath the Jew? or what profit is there of circumcision?" (Romans 3:1)

Paul raises the obvious objection. If the Jew is judged just like the Gentile, if law and circumcision do not rescue, then what advantage was there at all?

Paul's answer is strikingly restrained:

"Much every way: chiefly, because that unto them were committed the oracles of God." (Romans 3:2)

The advantage was not immunity. It was responsibility.

Israel was entrusted with God's words—not as a shield against judgment, but as a means of revelation for the world. Scripture was not given to excuse Israel; it was given to expose humanity and proclaim God's righteousness.

Privilege does not cancel accountability. It intensifies it.

God's Faithfulness Is Not Undermined by Human Failure

"For what if some did not believe? shall their unbelief make the faith of God without effect?" (Romans 3:3)

Paul confronts another evasion: If God's people failed, does that mean God failed?

His answer is unambiguous:

"God forbid: yea, let God be true, but every man a liar." (Romans 3:4)

Human sin does not weaken God's righteousness; it reveals it. God remains faithful even when His people are faithless. His judgments are just. His promises are not annulled by our rebellion.

Paul anticipates a perverse conclusion—that sin somehow glorifies God and therefore should be excused. He rejects it forcefully. God is not responsible for human unrighteousness, and His justice is not compromised by judging it.

At the edge of the road, every attempt to shift blame collapses.

The Universal Indictment

"What then? are we better than they? No, in no wise: for we have before proved both Jews and Gentiles, that they are all under sin." (Romans 3:9)

This sentence is the turning of the key.

Paul has finished arguing. He has proved his case. Jew and Gentile alike are not merely sinners; they are under sin—under its authority, its guilt, its dominion.

No group is elevated. No category escapes. The road has claimed everyone.

Scripture Speaks—and Closes Every Mouth

Paul now does something devastating: he lets Scripture speak.

He strings together a series of Old Testament citations—psalms and prophets—forming a single, relentless testimony:

"There is none righteous, no, not one."

"There is none that understandeth."

"There is none that seeketh after God."

"They are all gone out of the way."

"There is none that doeth good, no, not one."

This is not hyperbole. It is diagnosis.

Paul describes the whole man:

- mind: no understanding,

- will: no seeking,

- conduct: corruption,

- speech: deceit and violence,

- direction: no peace,

- posture: no fear of God.

This is not merely a list of extreme sinners. It is a portrait of humanity apart from grace.

The Scripture the Jew trusted as a badge now speaks as a witness against him. The Word of God does not flatter its hearers. It condemns them.

The Law's Final Work: Silence

"Now we know that what things soever the law saith, it saith to them who are under the law: that every mouth may be stopped, and all the

world may become guilty before God."
(Romans 3:19)

This is the end of the road.

The law has accomplished its purpose—not by justifying, but by silencing. No excuses remain. No comparisons help. No heritage protects. No ignorance pleads innocence.

Every mouth is stopped.

Not persuaded.

Not negotiated with.

Stopped.

The world does not stand accused by rumor or opinion, but by God Himself. Guilt is no longer debated. It is established.

No Ground Left Beneath Our Feet

"Therefore by the deeds of the law there shall no flesh be justified in his sight: for by the law is the knowledge of sin." (Romans 3:20)

This verse removes the final illusion: that obedience might eventually rescue us.

The law cannot justify because it was never designed to heal. It diagnoses. It exposes. It reveals sin—but it cannot remove it.

Proper behavior cannot erase past guilt. Future obedience cannot undo present condemnation. The law can tell us we are falling, but it cannot stop the fall.

The road ends here. And beyond it is nothing solid at all.

Summary

Romans 3:1–20 brings humanity to the end of the road. Privilege does not exempt, Scripture does not flatter, and law does not justify. Jew and Gentile alike are proven to be under sin. God's faithfulness stands firm, even as every human defense collapses. Scripture testifies unanimously: none are righteous, none seek God, none do good. The law speaks to silence every mouth and establish universal guilt. By the works of the law, no flesh will be justified. There is no ground left to stand on.

Application

1. Stop arguing with God's verdict.

The law was not given to negotiate innocence, but to establish guilt.

2. Abandon every refuge built on effort or identity.

   When the road ends, credentials do not become wings.

3. Let Scripture speak fully before you rush to comfort.

   Grace is only good news after the bad news has been allowed to finish.

4. Accept silence as mercy.

   A stopped mouth is closer to salvation than a self-defending one.

5. Do not look for footing where none exists.

   The end of the road is not the end of hope—but hope has not yet appeared.

Prayer

Father,

We stand silent before Your law. Every excuse has failed. Every comparison has collapsed. We confess that there is no righteousness in us, no ground beneath us, no defense left to offer. Shut our mouths where pride still speaks, and strip us of every false confidence. Teach us to feel the weight of guilt fully, that we might not diminish the glory of the rescue You are about to reveal. Keep us from leaping ahead of Your Word, and prepare our hearts for what only You can provide.

We pray to You,

In the name of Jesus Christ. Amen.

Fortress of Justification

8

But Now

But now the righteousness of God without the law is manifested, being witnessed by the law and the prophets;

Even the righteousness of God which is by faith of Jesus Christ unto all and upon all them that believe: for there is no difference:

For all have sinned, and come short of the glory of God;

Being justified freely by his grace through the redemption that is in Christ Jesus:

Whom God hath set forth to be a propitiation through faith in his blood, to declare his righteousness for the remission of sins that are past, through the forbearance of God;

To declare, I say, at this time his righteousness: that he might be just, and the justifier of him which believeth in Jesus. (Romans 3:21-26)

The road has ended. There is no more ground beneath human feet. The law has spoken, and every mouth has been stopped. No excuse remains, no identity protects, no effort redeems. Humanity stands guilty—not because God demanded too much, but because even the truth we possessed we did not obey.

And into that silence Paul speaks two words that signal not human movement, but divine action:

"But now."

These words do not announce a change in humanity. They announce a change in what is being revealed. The problem has never been that God's righteousness was unclear, but that it was resisted, misunderstood, or accused. Now God makes His righteousness unmistakably plain.

A Righteousness Made Manifest

"But now the righteousness of God without the law is manifested, being witnessed by the law and the prophets." (Romans 3:21)

Paul does not begin by speaking of what God gives to sinners. He begins with what God shows about Himself.

The righteousness now revealed is God's righteousness—His justice, faithfulness, and moral perfection—made visible in history. This righteousness is not produced by the law, yet it is not foreign to it. The law and the prophets have borne witness to it all along. What they could not accomplish, they anticipated.

The same Scriptures that condemned humanity now testify that God had always intended to act righteously on humanity's behalf—without compromising His holiness.

The drawbridge appears here, not because humanity discovered a way forward, but because God stepped into view.

Faith as Agreement with God's Truth

"Even the righteousness of God which is by faith of Jesus Christ unto all and upon all them

that believe: for there is no difference."
(Romans 3:22)

This righteousness becomes clear and compelling by faith.

Faith here is not first a mechanism of transfer; it is an act of trustful recognition. It is taking God at His word —about Himself, about us, and about the distance between. Faith agrees with God's verdict where pride once argued. It receives God's self-disclosure where self-justification once resisted.

There is no difference between Jew and Gentile because the problem was never access to information, but refusal of truth. Faith does not narrow the path; it opens the eyes.

The drawbridge is not crossed by understanding oneself differently, but by seeing God rightly.

Why the Revelation Is Necessary

"For all have sinned, and come short of the glory of God." (Romans 3:23)

Paul does not retreat from the indictment. He restates it.

The issue is not merely that we have broken rules, but that we have fallen short of God Himself. His glory is the standard. Anything less than perfect alignment with His character is failure.

This is why the righteousness revealed must be God's own. No human righteousness could ever span that gulf. The road did not end because effort ran out; it ended because the destination was unreachable by human means.

God Shown Righteous in Justifying

"Being justified freely by his grace through the redemption that is in Christ Jesus." (Romans 3:24)

Paul now introduces justification—but carefully.

Justification here is not yet explained in its full personal application. It is introduced as God's gracious action, grounded in redemption. It is free— not because it costs nothing, but because it is not earned.

The emphasis remains on God's initiative. The question being answered is not yet, "How do I receive righteousness?" but, "How can God righteously declare sinners right?"

The answer lies not in overlooking guilt, but in redemption.

The Cross as Public Vindication

"Whom God hath set forth to be a propitiation through faith in his blood, to declare his righteousness..." (Romans 3:25)

Here the center of the drawbridge comes fully into view.

God did not hide His solution. He set it forth—publicly, historically, unmistakably. The cross is not a private transaction; it is a declaration.

Propitiation means that God's righteous wrath against sin is satisfied, not dismissed. The wrath revealed in Romans 1 is not denied here—it is answered. God remains righteous because sin is judged. God remains merciful because the judgment falls where He has appointed.

Faith does not soften God's justice; it acknowledges that justice has been done.

God Just and the Justifier

"...to declare, I say, at this time his righteousness: that he might be just, and the justifier of him which believeth in Jesus." (Romans 3:25–26)

This is the summit of Paul's argument so far.

The cross reveals that God is just—His judgment of sin is real, righteous, and uncompromised. And it reveals that God is the justifier—He is righteous even as He declares sinners right.

The tension that haunted the road is resolved here. God does not save by lowering His standard. He saves by fulfilling it Himself.

How sinners come to stand in that righteousness will be unfolded next. For now, Paul insists on this: God's righteousness has been vindicated, and therefore God can be trusted.

The drawbridge holds because its weight rests on God's character, not ours.

Summary

Romans 3:21–26 marks the great turning point of the Epistle. After the law has silenced every defense, God reveals His own righteousness apart from the law, yet witnessed by it. This righteousness is made visible through the cross of Jesus Christ and recognized by faith that submits to God's truth. All have sinned and fallen short of God's glory, but God has publicly demonstrated His justice through propitiation, showing Himself to be both just and the justifier. The drawbridge appears where the road ended—not because humanity found a way, but because God revealed who He truly is.

Application

1. Let God define righteousness before you seek reassurance.

   Faith begins by agreeing with God, not by correcting Him.

2. Stop measuring yourself and start beholding God.

   The gulf is not discovered by introspection, but by revelation.

3. Trust a salvation that defends God's justice.

   A gospel that excuses sin cannot save sinners.

4. Rest in a righteousness that is first God's.

   Only a righteous God can be trusted to justify.

5. Do not rush past the revelation.

   Before asking what God gives, learn who God has shown Himself to be.

Prayer

Father,

We praise You for revealing Your righteousness where we could not defend ourselves. When every excuse was silenced and every claim collapsed, You showed Yourself faithful, just, and true. Grant us faith to agree with Your verdict—to see You as You have revealed Yourself, and to trust You wholly. Prepare our hearts to receive what You will yet unfold, and keep us resting not in ourselves, but in Your righteous character displayed in Jesus Christ.

We pray to You,

In the name of Jesus Christ. Amen.

Fortress of Justification

9

Boasting Excluded

Where is boasting then? It is excluded. By what law? of works? Nay: but by the law of faith.

Therefore we conclude that a man is justified by faith without the deeds of the law.

Is he the God of the Jews only? is he not also of the Gentiles? Yes, of the Gentiles also:

Seeing it is one God, which shall justify the circumcision by faith, and uncircumcision through faith.

Do we then make void the law through faith?
God forbid: yea, we establish the law. (Romans
3:27-31)

Romans 3:21–26 was the great unveiling. God's righteousness—His justice, His faithfulness, His moral perfection—has been manifested apart from the law, though witnessed by the law and the prophets. God has shown Himself to be just, and the justifier of the one who believes in Jesus.

And now Paul draws the first unavoidable consequence.

If salvation is established by God's righteous work—if redemption is in Christ, propitiation is through His blood, and justification rests on faith—then there is one human posture that cannot survive this gospel:

boasting.

This is not a minor pastoral footnote. It is the first evidence that a man has stopped trying to save himself. Where boasting lives, faith has not yet begun.

The Question That Ends Self-Congratulation

"Where is boasting then? It is excluded."
(Romans 3:27)

Paul does not say boasting is discouraged. He says it is **excluded**—shut out, locked out, barred from entry. Why? Because the entire structure of justification is designed to display God's righteousness, not man's achievement.

If God had established salvation as a ladder—do these works, keep these rules, accumulate this merit —then the climber could brag. Even if he admitted God helped him, he would still claim some share of the credit. He could point to his steps, his sacrifices, his discipline, his religious performance, his moral improvement.

But Paul has already shown that the road ends in guilt. No man reaches the standard. No man can satisfy wrath. No man can bridge the gulf. When the drawbridge appears, it is not a tool for the strong; it is rescue for the helpless. And rescue does not produce boasting. It produces gratitude, submission, and quiet amazement.

Boasting is excluded because the gospel is not a reward for the worthy. It is mercy for the condemned.

Not the Law of Works, but the Law of Faith

"By what law? of works? Nay: but by the law of faith." (Romans 3:27)

Paul uses the word *law* here in a different sense. He is not speaking of the Mosaic law as a code, but of a ruling principle—a governing rule of how a thing operates.

- The law of works says: do, and receive.

- The law of faith says: receive, because Another has done.

Faith is not a work. It is not a payment. It is not a moral accomplishment. Faith is the renunciation of self-salvation. It is the surrender that admits: I cannot satisfy God's righteousness; I cannot absorb His wrath; I cannot repair my guilt; I cannot make myself right.

The law of faith is the principle by which a sinner is brought to rest—not in himself, but in the righteous provision of God.

And once faith rules, boasting dies.

The Conclusion Paul Forces Upon Us

"Therefore we conclude that a man is justified by faith without the deeds of the law." (Romans 3:28)

Paul does not leave this as a suggestion. He calls it a conclusion. The entire argument from Romans 1 to this point has been moving toward this statement like a court case moving toward verdict.

- The Gentile cannot be justified by ignorance.

- The moral man cannot be justified by comparison.

- The Jew cannot be justified by possession of the law.

- The law cannot justify—because it reveals sin and silences excuses.

Therefore, justification must come another way.

Justification is not excusing sin. It is not pretending guilt does not exist. It is not God lowering His standard. It is God righteously dealing with guilt so that the sinner may stand before Him without condemnation.

And Paul's point here is simple and final: that standing does not come by "deeds of the law." It comes by faith.

One God, One Way

"Is he the God of the Jews only? is he not also of the Gentiles? Yes, of the Gentiles also." (Romans 3:29–30)

Here Paul presses the implication outward.

If justification were through the Jewish law as an achievement system, then salvation would be confined to the Jewish sphere. But Paul insists God is not tribal. He is not a local deity bound to one ethnic boundary or one cultural mechanism. He is the one God of all, and therefore He justifies all in one consistent way.

> *"Seeing it is one God, which shall justify the circumcision by faith, and uncircumcision through faith." (Romans 3:30)*

Paul uses two phrases— *"by faith"* and *"through faith"* —but his point is not two methods. It is one method applied to two groups. Whether covenant-marked or uncovenanted, whether insider or outsider, whether Jew or Gentile, there is one way a sinner stands justified:

faith.

And that destroys both pride and despair.

• Pride cannot claim special access.

• Despair cannot claim exclusion.

There is one God, and He is righteous to justify the one who believes.

Faith Does Not Void the Law—It Establishes It

"Do we then make void the law through faith? God forbid: yea, we establish the law." *(Romans 3:31)*

This is the anticipated objection: If justification is by faith, does that make the law irrelevant? Does it empty God's commands of meaning? Does it turn holiness into optional advice?

Paul's response is sharp: God forbid.

Faith does not destroy the law; it establishes it, because faith finally agrees with what the law has been saying all along:

• God's standard is righteous.

• Man has not kept it.

• Guilt is real.

• Judgment is just.

• The need for mercy is absolute.

The law is not nullified by faith—it is fulfilled in its intended work. It was never given as a ladder for sinners to climb into acceptance. It was given to expose sin, shut mouths, and make the world guilty—

so that salvation would be known as grace, not wages.

Faith establishes the law by admitting the law was right.

Summary

Romans 3:27–31 states the first consequence of God's righteousness revealed in the gospel: boasting is excluded. Justification does not come by the law of works—doing and earning—but by the law of faith—trusting and receiving. Therefore, a man is justified by faith apart from the deeds of the law. Because God is one, He is God of Jews and Gentiles alike and justifies both by faith. Far from voiding the law, faith establishes it by agreeing with its verdict and fulfilling its intended purpose.

Application

1. Identify where you still want credit.

    Boasting does not always sound like arrogance. Sometimes it sounds like self-reliance: "I've always tried," "I've done my best," "I'm not like them." The gospel excludes all of it.

2. Receive faith as surrender, not contribution.

Faith is not adding a spiritual work to your moral résumé. It is abandoning the résumé entirely.

3. Refuse ethnic, cultural, or religious superiority.

   If God justifies Jew and Gentile the same way, then no group can claim a higher standing than another.

4. Honor the law by agreeing with it.

   The law is established when you stop arguing and start confessing: God is right; I am not.

1. Let the end of boasting become the beginning of gratitude.

   A man who cannot boast in himself is finally free to rejoice in Christ.

Prayer

Father,

We confess how easily we seek something to boast in—our morality, our knowledge, our background, our discipline, even our religious habits. Shut the door on boasting in us, and teach us the law of faith: to receive what we could never earn, and to rest in what Christ has done. Thank You that You are God of Jew and Gentile alike, and that You justify sinners in a righteous way. Establish Your law in our hearts by bringing us to agreement with Your verdict, and make our lives a testimony not to our goodness, but to Your grace.

We pray to You,

In the name of Jesus Christ. Amen.

10

Counted Righteous

What shall we say then that Abraham our father, as pertaining to the flesh, hath found?

For if Abraham were justified by works, he hath whereof to glory; but not before God.

For what saith the scripture? Abraham believed God, and it was counted unto him for righteousness.

Now to him that worketh is the reward not reckoned of grace, but of debt.

But to him that worketh not, but believeth on him that justifieth the ungodly, his faith is counted for righteousness.

Even as David also describeth the blessedness of the man, unto whom God imputeth righteousness without works,

Saying, Blessed are they whose iniquities are forgiven, and whose sins are covered.

Blessed is the man to whom the Lord will not impute sin. (Romans 4:1-8)

Having excluded boasting, Paul now anticipates the most natural objection—especially from a Jewish reader: *If justification is by faith apart from works, then what about Abraham?*

Abraham is not a peripheral figure. He is the patriarch, the father of Israel, the man to whom the promises were given. If anyone could claim standing with God by achievement, obedience, or spiritual stature, surely it would be Abraham.

Paul turns to him precisely because he represents the strongest possible case for justification by works—and then dismantles it.

Abraham According to the Flesh

"What shall we say then that Abraham our father, as pertaining to the flesh, hath found?" (Romans 4:1)

Paul frames the question carefully. He asks what Abraham achieved according to the flesh—that is, by human effort, merit, or obedience.

"If Abraham were justified by works, he hath whereof to glory; but not before God." (Romans 4:2)

Paul concedes the point hypothetically. If Abraham's standing with God were based on works, then boasting would be legitimate. Abraham could point to obedience, sacrifice, endurance, and faithfulness. He could glory—before men.

But Paul adds a decisive qualifier: "but not before God."

Human admiration and divine verdict are not the same thing. What impresses men does not satisfy God's righteousness. Standing before God requires more than visible obedience; it requires perfect alignment with His will—and Abraham, like every other man, fell short.

Scripture's Verdict, Not Tradition's Assumption

"For what saith the scripture? Abraham believed God, and it was counted unto him for righteousness." (Romans 4:3)

Paul does not argue from sentiment or reputation. He argues from Scripture.

Genesis 15 does not say Abraham earned righteousness. It does not say righteousness grew gradually from obedience. It says righteousness was counted to him.

This word marks a turning point.

Paul introduces an accounting term—*logizomai*—to describe justification. Righteousness is not infused, discovered, or awakened. It is reckoned, credited, counted.

Abraham did not present God with righteousness. God credited righteousness to Abraham.

Wages or Gift

"Now to him that worketh is the reward not reckoned of grace, but of debt." (Romans 4:4)

Paul sharpens the contrast.

If justification operates on a works system, then righteousness is wages. God owes it. Grace disappears. Salvation becomes transaction, not mercy.

> *"But to him that worketh not, but believeth on him that justifieth the ungodly, his faith is counted for righteousness." (Romans 4:5)*

This sentence is deliberately unsettling.

God does not justify the righteous. He justifies the ungodly.

Faith here is not a work that earns righteousness. It is the empty hand that receives a verdict it did not deserve. Faith agrees with God's assessment—that the believer is ungodly and cannot pay the debt—and trusts God to act righteously anyway.

Justification is not God pretending sinners are righteous. It is God declaring them righteous on a just basis He Himself provides.

David's Witness: Blessed Without Works

Paul now calls a second witness—David.

> *"Even as David also describeth the blessedness of the man, unto whom God*

imputeth righteousness without works..."
(Romans 4:6)

David speaks not of reward, but of blessing.

"Blessed are they whose iniquities are forgiven,

And whose sins are covered.

Blessed is the man to whom the Lord will not impute sin." (Romans 4:7-8)

David does not describe a man who never sinned. He describes a man whose sin is not counted against him.

Here imputation works in two directions:

• Righteousness is counted to the believer.

• Sin is no longer counted against him.

The blessing David celebrates is not moral success, but gracious accounting. The ledger changes—not because the man paid the debt, but because God chose not to charge it.

What "Counted" Really Means

Paul's language leaves no room for ambiguity.

To count or impute is not to imagine something that isn't true. It is to assign a status based on a real and sufficient ground. The believer's account was genuinely in deficit. God does not ignore that deficit. He addresses it by crediting righteousness where it did not exist.

This is not fiction. It is mercy applied through justice.

Abraham believed. David rejoiced. And Paul insists this logic is not exceptional—it is foundational.

Summary

Romans 4:1–8 establishes that justification has never operated by works. Abraham was not justified by what he achieved according to the flesh, but by believing God, and righteousness was counted to him. Paul contrasts wages and grace, showing that God justifies the ungodly, not by debt, but by gift. David confirms this blessedness: sins forgiven, guilt covered, and sin no longer imputed. Justification is an act of divine accounting, grounded in grace and received by faith.

Application

1. Stop treating obedience as payment.

    Good works are fruits of faith, not currency for justification.

2. Let Scripture define how God saves.

   Tradition may admire Abraham's obedience; Scripture emphasizes his belief.

3. Rest in grace, not calculation.

   If righteousness is a gift, then anxiety about "earning enough" has no place.

4. Rejoice in forgiveness that changes the ledger.

   Blessed is the man whose sin is not counted—not the man who claims he has none.

5. Believe God where self-justification once spoke.

   Faith begins by agreeing with God's verdict and trusting His provision.

Prayer

Father,

We thank You that our standing with You is not a wage earned, but a gift received. Teach us to stop working for what You freely give, and to trust You where we once tried to justify ourselves. Thank You for counting righteousness where there was only debt, and for covering sin we could never erase. Grant us faith like Abraham's—to believe You—and joy like David's—to rest in forgiveness. May our lives reflect gratitude, not self-congratulation.

We pray to You,

In the name of Jesus Christ. Amen.

Fortress of Justification

11

Sealed,
Not Saved

Cometh this blessedness then upon the circumcision only, or upon the uncircumcision also? for we say that faith was reckoned to Abraham for righteousness.

How was it then reckoned? when he was in circumcision, or in uncircumcision? Not in circumcision, but in uncircumcision.

And he received the sign of circumcision, a seal of the righteousness of the faith which he had yet being uncircumcised: that he might be the father of all them that believe, though they be not circumcised; that righteousness might be imputed unto them also:

113

And the father of circumcision to them who are not of the circumcision only, but who also walk in the steps of that faith of our father Abraham, which he had being yet uncircumcised. (Romans 4:9-12)

Once Paul has established that righteousness is counted apart from works, he anticipates the next objection—one that moves from effort to identity.

If righteousness is counted by faith, then to whom does this blessing belong?

Is it reserved for those who bear the covenant mark? Or does it extend beyond those visible boundaries?

Paul returns again to Abraham, not as a theological abstraction, but as a historical man whose life provides a fixed timeline that cannot be rearranged.

The Question of Belonging

"Cometh this blessedness then upon the circumcision only, or upon the uncircumcision also?" (Romans 4:9)

Paul is not asking whether circumcision matters. He is asking whether it saves.

If the blessing of forgiveness and non-imputation of sin belongs only to the circumcised, then justification remains confined to a single ethnic and covenantal boundary. But if Abraham himself received this blessing before circumcision, then the boundary must be wider than the sign.

Paul answers by returning to Scripture—not speculation.

The Timing That Settles the Matter

"How was it then reckoned? when he was in circumcision, or in uncircumcision? Not in circumcision, but in uncircumcision." (Romans 4:10)

This is the hinge of Paul's argument.

Abraham was declared righteous in Genesis 15. Circumcision was instituted in Genesis 17. The order is not incidental; it is decisive.

Righteousness was counted to Abraham before the sign was given. Therefore, the sign cannot be the cause of justification. It follows justification; it does not produce it.

Paul does not diminish circumcision by saying this. He clarifies its purpose.

Sign and Seal, Not Source

"And he received the sign of circumcision, a seal of the righteousness of the faith which he had yet being uncircumcised..." (Romans 4:11)

Circumcision was a sign—a visible marker of belonging.

It was also a seal—a confirmation of something already true.

A seal does not create reality; it authenticates it. It does not generate righteousness; it testifies to it.

Abraham did not believe because he was circumcised. He was circumcised because he believed. His obedience was a response to grace, not a condition for it.

This distinction preserves both grace and obedience. Grace comes first. Obedience follows. When that order is reversed, the sign becomes a substitute for faith and the seal becomes a counterfeit savior.

Father of All Who Believe

"That he might be the father of all them that believe, though they be not circumcised..." (Romans 4:11)

Paul now draws the universal conclusion.

Abraham is not merely the father of the circumcised. He is the father of all who believe—Jew and Gentile alike—because his defining feature was not his mark, but his faith.

And he is father of the circumcision not merely because they share his flesh, but because they walk in the steps of the faith he had before circumcision.

Heritage without faith does not make one a child of Abraham. Faith without heritage does.

Obedience Has a Place—But Not the Throne

Paul's argument does not reduce obedience to irrelevance. It restores it to its proper place.

Circumcision mattered. It was commanded. It was meaningful. But it did not justify.

In the same way, outward acts of obedience in every age—baptism, confession, public profession, participation in worship—are signs and seals, not sources. They proclaim what God has done; they do not accomplish it.

When signs are mistaken for salvation, grace is eclipsed and faith is replaced by ritual. When signs follow faith, they become powerful witnesses to God's work.

Summary

Romans 4:9–12 clarifies the role of covenant signs in God's saving work. The blessing of forgiveness and righteousness does not belong only to the circumcised, because Abraham himself was declared righteous before circumcision. Circumcision was given as a sign and seal of the righteousness he already possessed by faith. Therefore, Abraham is the father of all who believe—both uncircumcised and circumcised—provided they walk in the steps of his faith. Obedience follows grace; it does not create it.

Application

1. Guard the order: faith first, obedience second.

    Whenever the order is reversed, the gospel is distorted.

2. Honor signs without trusting them.

    Outward marks testify to salvation; they do not produce it.

3. Refuse inherited faith without personal belief.

God has no grandchildren—only children who believe.

4. Let obedience flow from gratitude, not fear.

    A seal is joyfully received when the promise is already secure.

5. Walk in Abraham's steps, not merely his shadow.

    True belonging is shaped by faith, not flesh.

Prayer

Father,

We thank You that the blessing of forgiveness is not confined by outward marks, but granted through faith. Teach us to honor obedience without turning it into a substitute for grace. Guard us from trusting signs more than the Savior they point to. Give us hearts like Abraham's—to believe You first, and then to walk faithfully in response. May our obedience be a seal of gratitude, not an attempt to earn what You freely give.

We pray to You,

In the name of Jesus Christ. Amen.

12

Promise
by Faith,
That It Might Be by Grace

For the promise, that he should be the heir of the world, was not to Abraham, or to his seed, through the law, but through the righteousness of faith.

For if they which are of the law be heirs, faith is made void, and the promise made of none effect:

Because the law worketh wrath: for where no law is, there is no transgression.

Therefore it is of faith, that it might be by grace; to the end the promise might be sure to all the seed; not to that only which is of the law, but to that also which is of the faith of Abraham; who is the father of us all,

(As it is written, I have made thee a father of many nations,) before him whom he believed, even God, who quickeneth the dead, and calleth those things which be not as though they were. (Romans 4:13-17)

With Abraham firmly established as justified by faith apart from works, Paul now turns from signs to promises.

Circumcision clarified what does not justify.

Now Paul clarifies what does not secure inheritance.

The question before us is not merely how a man is forgiven, but how a promise given by God can ever be certain—especially when that promise stretches beyond one man, one nation, or one generation.

The Promise Was Never Law-Based

"For the promise, that he should be the heir of the world, was not to Abraham, or to his seed, through the law, but through the righteousness of faith." (Romans 4:13)

Paul makes a sweeping claim. The promise to Abraham was not simply about land, descendants, or national blessing. It was cosmic in scope: heir of the world. This promise could not have come through the law for a simple reason—the law did not yet exist.

Abraham lived centuries before Sinai. If the promise depended on law-keeping, then Abraham could never have received it, and neither could anyone after him. The promise rests instead on the righteousness of faith—that standing before God established by trusting Him.

The inheritance was never wages. It was always promise.

Law and Promise Cannot Share the Same Foundation

"For if they which are of the law be heirs, faith is made void, and the promise made of none effect." (Romans 4:14)

Paul does not say law and promise merely compete. He says they cancel one another.

If inheritance depends on law-keeping, then faith becomes unnecessary—and promise becomes meaningless. A promise assumes gift. Law assumes obligation. If inheritance is earned, it is no longer promised.

This is not an abstract theological tension. It is a logical impossibility. Law and promise cannot occupy the same ground. One must give way to the other.

Why the Law Can Never Secure Inheritance

"Because the law worketh wrath: for where no law is, there is no transgression." (Romans 4:15)

The law does not create blessing. It exposes guilt.

Paul does not criticize the law here; he defines its function. The law clarifies transgression. It does not remove it. Where law speaks, accountability increases—and wrath follows where obedience fails.

If inheritance depends on the law, then inheritance collapses under the weight of human sin. Instead of securing the promise, the law guarantees condemnation.

A promise that depends on law is a promise designed to fail.

Faith Chosen So Grace Might Reign

"Therefore it is of faith, that it might be by grace; to the end the promise might be sure to all the seed..." (Romans 4:16)

This is the heart of Paul's argument.

Faith is not chosen because it is easier. It is chosen because it is the only means compatible with grace. And grace is necessary if the promise is to be sure.

Law creates uncertainty—because it depends on performance. Grace creates certainty—because it depends on God.

If inheritance rests on faith, then it rests on grace.

If it rests on grace, then it rests on God.

If it rests on God, then it is secure.

And because it rests on faith rather than law, the promise extends beyond ethnic boundaries—to "all the seed," both those under the law and those who share Abraham's faith.

The God Who Makes Promise Possible

"As it is written, I have made thee a father of many nations, before him whom he believed,

even God, who quickeneth the dead, and calleth those things which be not as though they were." (Romans 4:17)

Paul ends this section not by describing Abraham, but by describing God.

Faith does not rest on optimism. It rests on the nature of the One who promises. Abraham believed a God who gives life to the dead and speaks reality into existence.

This is crucial. The promise did not depend on Abraham's capacity, fertility, strength, or longevity. It depended entirely on God's creative power. God did not wait for circumstances to cooperate; He spoke into impossibility.

That is the God faith trusts—and that is why the promise could never be law-based.

Summary

Romans 4:13–17 explains why God's promise to Abraham could never rest on law, but only on faith. The promise of inheritance preceded the law and would be void if it depended on law-keeping. The law exposes transgression and produces wrath, not certainty. Therefore, the promise is received by faith so that it may be grounded in grace and made sure to all who believe. This promise rests on the character of

God Himself—the One who gives life to the dead and calls into existence what does not yet exist.

Application

1. Do not place promise where performance rules.

   If blessing depends on you, it will never be sure.

2. Let grace carry the weight of certainty.

   Faith is secure only because grace rests on God's character.

3. Refuse any gospel that mixes inheritance with earning.

   What law secures today, it condemns tomorrow.

4. Trust the God who speaks into impossibility.

   Faith is not confidence in outcomes, but confidence in God.

5. Rest in a promise that cannot fail.

   What God grounds in grace cannot be undone by weakness.

Prayer

Father,

We thank You that Your promise does not depend on our strength, obedience, or consistency, but on Your grace and faithfulness. Teach us to rest where You have chosen to anchor our hope—not in law that exposes our failure, but in faith that trusts Your word. Strengthen us to believe You as Abraham did, trusting the God who gives life to the dead and calls into being what does not yet exist. Make us people who live by promise, not performance.

We pray to You,

In the name of Jesus Christ. Amen.

13

Against Hope, Believed in Hope

Who against hope believed in hope, that he might become the father of many nations, according to that which was spoken, So shall thy seed be.

And being not weak in faith, he considered not his own body now dead, when he was about an hundred years old, neither yet the deadness of Sarah's womb:

He staggered not at the promise of God through unbelief; but was strong in faith, giving glory to God;

And being fully persuaded that, what he had promised, he was able also to perform.

And therefore it was imputed to him for righteousness.

Now it was not written for his sake alone, that it was imputed to him;

But for us also, to whom it shall be imputed, if we believe on him that raised up Jesus our Lord from the dead;

Who was delivered for our offences, and was raised again for our justification. (Romans 4:18-25)

Paul has shown that righteousness is counted by faith, not earned by works; that covenant signs seal what faith receives; and that the promise rests on grace so it may be sure. Now he returns to Abraham one final time—not to rehearse doctrine, but to display faith in motion.

Romans 4:18–25 is not a new argument. It is the lived shape of everything Paul has said. Abraham's faith is no abstraction. It is trust exercised when circumstances deny the promise, when strength is gone, and when the future looks closed.

This is faith against hope—not wishful thinking, but confidence in God when visible reasons for confidence have disappeared.

Hope Where Hope Is Gone

"Who against hope believed in hope, that he might become the father of many nations..." *(Romans 4:18)*

Abraham did not believe because circumstances improved. He believed when circumstances contradicted the promise. Human hope—hope rooted in probability, biology, and timelines—had expired. Abraham was as good as dead, and Sarah's womb shared that verdict.

Yet Abraham believed in hope—not the hope of favorable odds, but the hope anchored in God's word. His faith did not deny reality; it trusted God over reality.

The promise did not rest on Abraham's potential. It rested on God's power.

Faith That Faces the Facts

"And being not weak in faith, he considered not his own body now dead... neither yet the deadness of Sarah's womb." (Romans 4:19)

Paul is careful here. Abraham did not ignore the facts. He considered them. He knew his age. He knew Sarah's barrenness. Faith is not denial; it is evaluation with God in view.

Weak faith pretends obstacles do not exist. Strong faith looks straight at them and still trusts God.

Abraham's faith did not grow because the situation softened. It grew because God remained faithful.

No Staggering at the Promise

"He staggered not at the promise of God through unbelief; but was strong in faith, giving glory to God." (Romans 4:20)

To stagger is to hesitate between trust and doubt, to lean forward and then pull back. Abraham did not stagger—not because he never struggled, but because he did not ultimately retreat.

Faith gives glory to God by refusing to treat God's promises as fragile. Abraham honored God by trusting Him to be who He said He was.

"And being fully persuaded that, what he had promised, he was able also to perform." *(Romans 4:21)*

Faith rests not in desire, but in persuasion—confidence that God's ability matches His word. Abraham did not know how God would act. He knew who God was.

Why Righteousness Was Counted

"And therefore it was imputed to him for righteousness." (Romans 4:22)

The word *therefore* matters.

Righteousness was not counted because Abraham achieved moral perfection. It was counted because Abraham trusted God at the point where self-sufficiency was impossible. Faith did not impress God; it agreed with Him.

Imputation follows faith because faith abandons every competing claim to righteousness.

Not for Abraham Alone—But for Us

"Now it was not written for his sake alone, that it was imputed to him; but for us also..." *(Romans 4:23)*

Here Paul turns the spotlight directly onto the reader.

Abraham's story is not preserved as an ancient curiosity. It is written for us. The same accounting logic applies. The same God justifies. The same righteousness is counted.

> *"To whom it shall be imputed, if we believe on him that raised up Jesus our Lord from the dead." (Romans 4:24)*

The object of faith is now explicit. Faith is not generic trust in God's power. It is trust in the God who raises the dead—specifically, the God who raised Jesus.

Abraham believed that God could bring life from death. We believe that God has done so.

Faith Anchored in the Resurrection

> *"Who was delivered for our offences, and was raised again for our justification." (Romans 4:25)*

Paul ends the chapter by tying everything together.

• Christ was delivered because of our offenses—our guilt required judgment.

- Christ was raised for our justification—His resurrection declares that judgment has been satisfied.

The resurrection is not an appendix to the cross. It is God's public declaration that the sacrifice was accepted, that righteousness was upheld, and that justification is secure.

Faith does not merely look backward to the cross; it looks forward to the risen Christ.

Summary

Romans 4:18–25 completes Paul's use of Abraham by showing faith under impossibility. Abraham believed God against all human hope, fully persuaded of God's power to perform what He promised. Therefore righteousness was counted to him. This account was written not for Abraham alone, but for all who believe in the God who raised Jesus from the dead. Christ was delivered for our offenses and raised for our justification, anchoring faith not in human strength, but in resurrection power.

Application

1. Do not wait for circumstances to support faith.

   Faith often begins where visible hope ends.

2. Face reality honestly—and trust God anyway.

   Strong faith does not ignore weakness; it trusts God beyond it.

3. Let God's character carry the promise.

   Faith is persuasion about who God is, not certainty about outcomes.

4. Receive righteousness as a counted gift.

   Imputation follows faith, not effort.

5. Anchor faith in the risen Christ.

   Justification rests not only on a death endured, but on a life raised.

Prayer

Father,

We thank You for the faith of Abraham, not as a model of human strength, but as a witness to Your faithfulness. Teach us to trust You when hope runs out, to face our weakness honestly, and to rest fully in Your power to give life from death. Thank You that this righteousness was counted not for Abraham alone, but for us who believe in You who raised Jesus from the dead. Establish our faith in the risen Christ, and prepare us to live in the peace that justification brings.

We pray to You,

In the name of Jesus Christ. Amen.

Fortress of Justification

14

Life Inside the Walls

Therefore being justified by faith, we have peace with God through our Lord Jesus Christ:

By whom also we have access by faith into this grace wherein we stand, and rejoice in hope of the glory of God. (Romans 5:1-2)

Romans 5 marks a decisive shift in Paul's argument. Up to this point, the question has been judicial:

How can a righteous God justify the ungodly?

That question has now been answered. Christ has propitiated God's wrath. Righteousness has been revealed. Faith has been counted. Boasting has been excluded. The verdict has been rendered.

Now Paul turns to a new question:

What does life look like once justification has been accomplished?

Romans 5 does not explain how to be justified. It assumes justification and explores its results. The believer is no longer on the road, no longer standing at the edge of judgment, no longer pleading a case. He has entered. He is inside.

Peace, Access, and Standing

"Therefore being justified by faith, we have peace with God through our Lord Jesus Christ:

By whom also we have access by faith into this grace wherein we stand, and rejoice in hope of the glory of God." (Romans 5:1–2)

Justification produces peace—not merely an inner feeling, but the objective end of hostility. The war between God and man is over. The rebel has surrendered and been received, not as a prisoner, but as a son.

This peace is not achieved by effort, nor maintained by vigilance. It is the settled result of Christ's work. The walls now stand between the believer and every enemy that once pursued him.

Through Christ, we also have access. The word carries the sense of being escorted—drawn safely into a place we could never reach on our own. Christ does not merely open the door; He brings us through it.

And having entered, Paul says we stand. This is not a probationary foothold. It is a fixed position. Grace is no longer something we approach; it is the ground beneath our feet.

Rejoicing Within the Walls

"And not only so, but we glory in tribulations also: knowing that tribulation worketh patience;

And patience, experience; and experience, hope:

And hope maketh not ashamed; because the love of God is shed abroad in our hearts by the Holy Ghost which is given unto us." (Romans 5:3–5)

Life inside the walls does not eliminate suffering. It redefines it.

Paul does not say we endure tribulation grimly, or tolerate it reluctantly. He says we rejoice—not because pain is pleasant, but because it is purposeful. Everything that happens to the justified person happens within the field of God's grace.

Tribulation produces endurance. Endurance produces tested character. Tested character produces hope. This is not theoretical optimism. It is the confidence that God is shaping His people for what lies ahead.

And this hope does not disappoint, because it rests on love—God's love poured out, not emotionally, but decisively, into the very seat of our will by the Holy Ghost. The forging does not destroy us, because it is governed by love.

Love Demonstrated, Not Declared

"For when we were yet without strength, in due time Christ died for the ungodly.

For scarcely for a righteous man will one die: yet peradventure for a good man some would even dare to die.

But God commendeth his love toward us, in that, while we were yet sinners, Christ died for us." (Romans 5:6–8)

Paul now explains why hope does not disappoint. God's love is not inferred. It is demonstrated.

Christ did not die for righteous men. He did not wait for repentance, reform, or readiness. He died for the ungodly—those living as though God were irrelevant.

The love of God is not proven by what He says, but by what He has done. While rebellion was still active, Christ was sent to die. This is love beyond comparison, love that rewrites every human category of worth.

From Wrath to Reconciliation

"Much more then, being now justified by his blood, we shall be saved from wrath through him.

For if, when we were enemies, we were reconciled to God by the death of his Son, much more, being reconciled, we shall be saved by his life.

And not only so, but we also joy in God through our Lord Jesus Christ, by whom we have now received the atonement." (Romans 5:9–11)

Justification saves us from wrath. Reconciliation restores us to fellowship.

Christ's death accomplished a once-for-all judicial work. Christ's living ministry sustains a continuing relational one. The believer does not merely escape judgment; he enters fellowship.

We do not merely rejoice about God. We rejoice in God.

Two Men, Two Reigns

"Wherefore, as by one man sin entered into the world, and death by sin; and so death passed upon all men, for that all have sinned..." (Romans 5:12)

Paul now widens the lens. Justification cannot be fully understood unless we understand representation.

Adam was not merely the first sinner. He was the head of humanity. His sin introduced death, not only because all would later sin individually, but because all sinned in him. Death reigned from Adam onward, even where no revealed law existed.

Adam, Paul says, was "the figure of him that was to come."

But the reigns are not equal.

"For if by one man's offence death reigned by one; much more they which receive abundance of grace and of the gift of righteousness shall reign in life by one, Jesus Christ." (Romans 5:15)

Outside of Christ, death reigns.

Inside of Christ, believers reign.

Grace does not merely reverse Adam's failure; it overwhelms it.

Condemnation Replaced by Life

"Therefore as by the offence of one judgment came upon all men to condemnation; even so by the righteousness of one the free gift came upon all men unto justification of life." (Romans 5:18)

Just as condemnation came through one representative act, justification comes through another. Humanity's story turns not on effort, but on headship.

Adam's disobedience constituted many sinners.

Christ's obedience constitutes many righteous.

And now grace reigns—not by ignoring sin, but by triumphing over it through righteousness unto eternal life.

Summary

Romans 5 reveals life inside the walls of justification. Peace replaces hostility. Grace becomes the believer's standing. Suffering is reinterpreted as formation. God's love is demonstrated decisively in Christ's death. And humanity itself is shown to stand under one of two reigns: Adam's reign of death, or Christ's reign of life.

Application

1. Live as one who is no longer at war with God.

    Peace with God is settled, not fragile.

2. Interpret suffering through grace, not fear.

    Nothing reaches you outside God's walls.

3. Anchor hope in God's demonstrated love.

    Christ's death is the guarantee.

4. Remember whose reign you are under.

    Grace now reigns unto life.

5. Prepare for what God is forming you to become.

    This life is training for glory.

Prayer

Father,

We thank You that through Jesus Christ we now have peace with You. Thank You that we stand in grace, that Your love has been demonstrated beyond question, and that death no longer reigns over us. Teach us to live as those who are inside the walls— secure, formed by Your hand, and rejoicing in the hope of Your glory.

We pray to You,,

In the name of Jesus Christ. Amen.

Fortress of Justification

15

Dead to
Sin, Alive to God

Romans 6 begins with a question that could only be asked after Romans 5 has been fully understood—and dangerously misunderstood. If grace reigns where sin abounded, if justification is complete and irreversible, if righteousness is a gift and not a wage—then why not sin freely and let grace abound?

Paul raises the objection himself because he knows the human heart. Whenever grace is preached clearly, someone will accuse it of producing moral laxity. Paul does not soften grace to prevent abuse. He defends it by explaining its power.

Romans 6 is not a call to try harder. It is a declaration that something decisive has already happened.

The Unthinkable Question

"What shall we say then? Shall we continue in sin, that grace may abound?

God forbid. How shall we, that are dead to sin, live any longer therein?" (Romans 6:1–2)

Paul's answer is immediate and forceful, because the suggestion itself is unthinkable. The question assumes that the believer remains alive to sin, still capable of continuing in it as though nothing decisive has occurred. Paul rejects that assumption outright. He does not ask, How should we who ought to die to sin live in it? He asks, How shall we who are dead to sin live in it? The distinction is crucial. Sanctification is not built on increased effort or moral resolve, but on a prior, irreversible reality. Its foundation is not striving. It is death.

Baptized into Christ's Death

"Know ye not, that so many of us as were baptized into Jesus Christ were baptized into his death?

Therefore we are buried with him by baptism into death: that like as Christ was raised up from the dead by the glory of the Father, even so we also should walk in newness of life." *(Romans 6:3–4)*

Paul appeals to something his readers already know, though they may not be fully living in light of it. Baptism does not save; it testifies. It is the visible confession that a believer has been united to Christ in His death, burial, and resurrection. To be baptized into Christ is to be publicly identified with a death that has already occurred. The old life has been buried, and a new life has begun.

Baptism functions like a grave marker rather than a starting line. It does not cause the death; it declares it. When a name is carved into stone, it does not kill the person—it announces that the death has already taken place. In the same way, baptism announces that the believer's former life has ended. The man who lived for himself has been laid in the ground with Christ, and the one who rises from the water does so as someone new.

Christianity, therefore, does not reform the old man or offer him better habits. It does not polish what God has condemned. It replaces him.

United with Him

"For if we have been planted together in the likeness of his death, we shall be also in the likeness of his resurrection." (Romans 6:5)

Union with Christ is the central reality of the Christian life. If we share in His death, we will share in His resurrection—not as a possibility, but as a certainty. The same union that justifies the sinner also sanctifies the believer. These are not separate stages of Christian experience, but inseparable expressions of the same living connection to Christ Himself.

The life now growing within the believer is not an improved version of the old, fallen life. It is resurrection life—life of a kind that did not exist before Christ broke the power of death. A corpse does not need rehabilitation; it needs resurrection. In the same way, God does not take the old man and make him manageable or respectable. He brings forth an entirely new life, animated by the power that raised Jesus from the grave. What emerges is not moral renovation, but new creation life, sustained by union with the risen Christ.

The Old Man Crucified

"Knowing this, that our old man is crucified with him, that the body of sin might be destroyed, that henceforth we should not serve sin.

For he that is dead is freed from sin." (Romans 6:6–7)

Paul does not say the old man is wounded, restrained, or re-educated. He says he is crucified.

The purpose of this crucifixion is liberation. Sin no longer has rightful authority. The chains have been broken.

A dead man is no longer a slave.

Life Beyond Death

"Now if we be dead with Christ, we believe that we shall also live with him:

Knowing that Christ being raised from the dead dieth no more; death hath no more dominion over him.

For in that he died, he died unto sin once: but in that he liveth, he liveth unto God." (Romans 6:8–10)

Christ's death was once for all, and His resurrection life is permanent. He does not die repeatedly, nor does He return to the grave. This matters because the believer's life is now bound up with His. What is true of Christ has become determinative for those united to Him. Death no longer reigns, and sin no longer holds rightful mastery.

Sanctification, therefore, is not the effort of forcing a dead system to behave as though it were alive. It is the outworking of a new life already present. When a healthy organ is transplanted, the body does not will it to function; it lives because it has been joined to a living source. In the same way, the believer's growth in holiness flows from union with Christ's resurrection life. Sin may still irritate and inflame like a lingering disease, but it no longer defines the organism. Sanctification is not the creation of life where none exists, but the maturation of life that has already been given.

Reckoning the Truth

"Likewise reckon ye also yourselves to be dead indeed unto sin, but alive unto God through Jesus Christ our Lord." (Romans 6:11)

Here is the first command of sanctification—and it is not do, but reckon. To reckon is to count something as true because God has declared it so. It is not self-deception or positive thinking; it is faith brought to bear on daily life. Reckoning does not create a new reality. It submits the mind and will to a reality that already exists by God's decree.

This is why the believer must learn to live according to who he is, not who he once was. A man who has been legally adopted does not become a son by acting like one; he acts like a son because he already is one. In the same way, the Christian does not pursue holiness in order to become dead to sin. He learns to think, choose, and live as someone whom God has already declared dead to sin and alive to Himself in Christ.

Summary

Romans 6:1–11 teaches that sanctification flows from union with Christ. The believer has died to sin, been buried with Christ, and raised to new life. Sin no longer reigns because death has already occurred. The Christian life is not the struggle of a sinner trying to be righteous, but the obedience of one who is already alive to God.

Application

1. Stop arguing with what God has declared dead.

    You cannot resurrect what God has crucified.

2. Live from identity, not aspiration.

    You are not becoming dead to sin—you are.

3. Let baptism shape daily obedience.

    It is a lifelong confession, not a past event.

4. Reckon before you resist.

    Victory flows from believing the truth.

5. Walk in resurrection life now.

    This life is preparation for eternal life.

Prayer

Father,

We thank You that in Jesus Christ we have died to sin and been raised to new life. Teach us to reckon what You have declared true, to live according to the life You have given, and to walk in the freedom Christ purchased for us. May our lives reflect resurrection reality, not graveyard habits.

We pray to You,

In the name of Jesus Christ. Amen.

Fortress of Justification

16

Under Grace, Not Under Sin

Romans 6 has been carefully ordered. Paul has already established what is true of the believer before he ever addresses what the believer must do.

• You are dead to sin.

• You are alive to God.

• You are united with Christ.

Only now does Paul turn to conduct—not as a threat, but as a consequence.

Sanctification is not the attempt to become something new. It is the daily refusal to live as something old.

A Command Grounded in Reality

"Let not sin therefore reign in your mortal body, that ye should obey it in the lusts thereof.

Neither yield ye your members as instruments of unrighteousness unto sin: but yield yourselves unto God, as those that are alive from the dead, and your members as instruments of righteousness unto God."
(Romans 6:12–13)

Paul does not say that sin will reign; he commands the believer not to let it reign. Sin is no longer a king by right. Its throne has been overturned, and it can rule only where it is invited. The believer still lives in a mortal body, still subject to weakness, appetite, and temptation, but sin no longer possesses legitimate authority over that body.

The issue, therefore, is not sin's presence, but its presentation. To yield is to place something at another's disposal. Paul frames the Christian life as a series of daily presentations—moments in which the believer offers himself either to sin or to God. The imagery is not accidental. Like a servant choosing whom to hand the keys of the house to, the believer determines who will exercise influence within. Holiness does not happen by accident, and sin does not rule by inevitability. One does not drift into righteousness, but neither is one dragged helplessly into rebellion. Each day, the believer presents himself, and that presentation reveals whom he is allowing to govern his life.

Grace Ends Sin's Dominion

"For sin shall not have dominion over you: for ye are not under the law, but under grace." *(Romans 6:14)*

This is not a command. It is a promise.

Sin's power is broken not by stricter rules, but by a new reign. The law could expose sin, condemn sin, and restrain sin—but it could not dethrone it.

Grace does.

To be under grace is not to be without obligation. It is to be under a different authority—one that produces obedience from life rather than fear.

Grace Is Not Permission

"What then? shall we sin, because we are not under the law, but under grace? God forbid.

Know ye not, that to whom ye yield yourselves servants to obey, his servants ye are to whom ye obey; whether of sin unto death, or of

obedience unto righteousness?" (Romans
6:15–16)

Paul anticipates the abuse of grace once again, and he rejects it just as forcefully. Grace does not erase consequences; it redefines allegiance. The gospel does not remove the concept of service from human life—it relocates it. Everyone serves something. The question is not whether you are a servant, but whose servant you are.

Sin markets itself as freedom, but it pays wages in death. Its promises are immediate and persuasive, yet its end is always the same. Obedience, by contrast, may appear costly in the moment, but it leads to life and produces righteousness. The difference is not merely moral, but directional. Like two roads diverging from the same starting point, both invite commitment, but only one leads where it claims to go. Grace does not free the believer from obedience; it frees him to obey the One whose service leads to life.

A Changed Allegiance

"But God be thanked, that ye were the servants
of sin, but ye have obeyed from the heart that
form of doctrine which was delivered you.

Being then made free from sin, ye became the servants of righteousness." (Romans 6:17–18)

Paul does not deny the past; he acknowledges it plainly. Ye were the servants of sin. The old mastery was real, and the bondage was genuine. But something decisive has happened. A new obedience has begun—one that is not coerced from the outside, but rendered from the heart. The believer has been transferred from one mastery to another.

Freedom from sin, therefore, does not mean independence. It means a new enslavement—one that leads to life. The gospel does not abolish lordship; it replaces a cruel master with a righteous one. Like a captive liberated from a tyrant only to be placed under the protection of a good king, the believer does not move into lawlessness, but into ordered freedom. What once destroyed now gives way to obedience that heals, sustains, and ultimately brings life.Slavery

That Leads to Life

"I speak after the manner of men because of the infirmity of your flesh..." (Romans 6:19–22)

Paul uses human categories to explain divine realities. Just as the believer once yielded his life to sin—progressively, habitually, and destructively—so now he is to yield himself to righteousness, progressively, intentionally, and completely. The point is not merely that actions have changed, but that direction has changed. Sin never stands still, and neither does sanctification. Both advance by accumulation, shaping the person over time.

The outcome of the old life was shame and death. The end was not accidental; it was the natural result of the path being walked. By contrast, the outcome of the new life is holiness and eternal life. Like two fields planted with different seeds, each grows according to its nature and yields a harvest consistent with what was sown. Paul's warning and encouragement are the same: what you continually present yourself to will determine what your life ultimately becomes.

Two Payoffs, Two Destinies

"For the wages of sin is death; but the gift of God is eternal life through Jesus Christ our Lord." (Romans 6:23)

This verse is often used evangelistically—and rightly so—but in this context Paul is addressing believers. His point is not that sin suddenly stops paying wages once a person is justified. Sin still pays wages. Grace still gives gifts.

For the unbeliever, the wages of sin culminate in eternal death, separation from God without remedy or end. But sin is no less lethal in the life of the believer. Though it can no longer condemn, it can still destroy. Sin kills joy, erodes testimony, fractures fellowship, and poisons peace. It wastes years, diminishes spiritual fruitfulness, and leaves wreckage in relationships. Given time, sin even takes its toll on the body itself, as patterns of rebellion manifest in stress, addiction, bitterness, and decay. Sin always pays in death; it never changes its currency.

Grace, by contrast, does not operate on a wage system at all. Eternal life is not earned through improved behavior or sustained obedience. It is the free gift of God in Jesus Christ our Lord. And that gift is not only future in its fulfillment, but present in its power. Life under grace is a life that grows—toward holiness, toward wholeness, toward communion with God. What sin corrodes, grace restores. What sin drains, grace supplies.

The contrast could not be sharper. Wages are earned. They are paid out in proportion to service rendered. Gifts, however, are given freely, not because of merit, but because of generosity. To live under sin is to labor for a master who always pays in death. To live under grace is to receive life—now in its transforming power, and finally in its eternal fullness.

Summary

Romans 6:12–23 completes Paul's argument on sanctification. The believer, having died with Christ and been raised to new life, must now choose daily whom he will serve. Sin no longer reigns, but it still seeks a throne. Grace does not excuse sin; it empowers obedience. The Christian life is a life of yielded allegiance under a new and gracious Master.

Application

1. Do not confuse grace with neutrality.

   You always serve someone.

2. Present yourself deliberately.

   Sanctification is practiced one decision at a time.

3. Remember who reigns.

   Sin has no rightful claim over you.

4. Expect progress, not perfection.

   Yielding produces growth.

5. Live for the gift, not the wages.

   Only one leads to life.

Prayer

Father,

We thank You that sin no longer has dominion over us, and that we now live under grace. Teach us to yield ourselves to You daily, to refuse sin's false promises, and to live as servants of righteousness. May our lives bear the fruit of holiness and reflect the gift of eternal life You have given us through Jesus Christ.

We pray to You,

In the name of Jesus Christ. Amen.

Fortress of Justification

17

The
Enemy
Within the Walls

Romans 7 is not a retreat from the freedom of Romans 6, nor a contradiction of the victory announced there. It is an explanation. Paul has declared that believers are dead to sin and not under the law but under grace (Romans 6:14). That declaration raises an unavoidable question— especially for those who know the law:

If we are justified apart from the law, what is now our relationship to it?

And if sin no longer reigns, why did obedience under the law feel like bondage?

Romans 7 answers both questions by exposing what the law can do—and what it cannot. The law is holy, just, and good. But the law was never given to produce righteousness in fallen flesh. When righteousness is pursued by obligation rather than surrender, even obedience becomes a form of rebellion. And that is the tragedy Paul describes.

This chapter is not written to excuse Christian defeat. It is written to destroy confidence in law-keeping as a means of pleasing God, and to prepare the reader for life in the Spirit.

The Law's Dominion Ends at Death

> "Know ye not, brethren, (for I speak to them that know the law,) how that the law hath dominion over a man as long as he liveth?" (Romans 7:1)

Paul addresses those who "know the law." He is not speaking to moral outsiders, but to religious insiders —particularly Jewish believers who still assumed that covenant faithfulness meant continuing submission to the Mosaic law as a governing authority.

The principle Paul states is simple: law has authority only while a person lives. Legal claims end at death.

He illustrates with marriage. A woman is bound to her husband while he lives; death dissolves the legal bond. Once death occurs, the law governing that relationship no longer applies.

The illustration is not about marriage ethics. It is about jurisdiction. Death ends legal dominion.

Dead to the Law by the Body of Christ

"Wherefore, my brethren, ye also are become dead to the law by the body of Christ..." (Romans 7:4)

Paul now applies the principle directly. Believers have died to the law—not because the law was evil, but because death changes standing. In union with Christ's death, the believer has passed beyond the law's covenant authority.

This is decisive. Paul does not say the law died. He says we died—"by the body of Christ." The believer's relationship to the law has ended at the cross.

But death is not the goal. Transfer is.

"...that ye should be married to another, even to him who is raised from the dead, that we should bring forth fruit unto God."

Freedom from the law is not freedom from obligation; it is freedom for union. The believer now belongs to the risen Christ. Fruit is still required—but it is fruit produced by life, not demanded by statute.

When the Law Meets Flesh

"For when we were in the flesh, the motions of sins, which were by the law, did work in our members to bring forth fruit unto death." *(Romans 7:5)*

Paul describes life "in the flesh"—life governed by fallen human nature. When the law encounters flesh, sin seizes the commandment as an opportunity. The law does not create sin; it exposes and provokes it.

Commands restrain behavior, but they cannot change desire. The flesh may comply outwardly while remaining inwardly hostile to God. As a result, even law-keeping can produce "fruit unto death."

"But now we are delivered from the law... that we should serve in newness of spirit, and not in the oldness of the letter." *(Romans 7:6)*

Deliverance from the law does not produce lawlessness. It produces new service—service animated by the Spirit rather than compelled by external command. Paul has now set the contrast that governs the rest of the chapter: letter versus Spirit, flesh versus life.

The Law Vindicated

Paul anticipates the objection: "Is the law sin?" His answer is immediate and absolute—"God forbid."

The law reveals sin. It names what the flesh would excuse. Paul uses coveting as an example: without the commandment, desire hides itself; with the commandment, sin is exposed as rebellion.

> *"Wherefore the law is holy, and the commandment holy, and just, and good." (Romans 7:12)*

The law is not the problem. Sin is.

But the law has a function: it makes sin "exceeding sinful." It strips away illusion. It leaves the sinner without refuge in self-justification. What the law cannot do is deliver.

And it is at this point that Paul turns inward.

Saul of Tarsus: Law Without the Spirit

> *"For we know that the law is spiritual: but I am carnal, sold under sin." (Romans 7:14)*

Paul does not downgrade the law. He indicts the flesh. The law is spiritual—it addresses the heart and requires submission. The flesh cannot do that.

The man Paul describes here is not indifferent to God. He delights in the law. He strives to obey it. Yet he is enslaved.

This description fits precisely what we know of Saul of Tarsus.

Before Christ, Saul was a Pharisee—zealous, disciplined, outwardly blameless. He persecuted believers, convinced he was serving God. Yet the risen Christ said to him, "It is hard for thee to kick against the pricks." Saul was resisting conviction while pursuing righteousness by law.

"I do what I hate."

Not because he wanted to serve God but was too weak—but because he hated the obligation of obedience while submitting to it for the sake of righteousness. His actions and desires were divided. His obedience was real, but it was not worship.

This is law-keeping without the Spirit.

The law restrained his behavior, but it could not transform his heart. His struggle was not between Spirit and flesh, but between conviction and pride, command and autonomy.

"O wretched man that I am! who shall deliver me from the body of this death?" (Romans 7:24)

This is not the cry of sanctification frustration. It is the collapse of self-trust. Saul does not ask, "What shall I do?" He asks, "Who shall deliver me?"

"I thank God through Jesus Christ our Lord." (Romans 7:25)

Deliverance does not come through deeper discipline or stricter obedience. It comes through a Person. The law exposes the need. Christ provides the rescue.

Summary

Romans 7 explains why the law cannot sanctify fallen humanity. The law's dominion ends at death, and believers have died to the law through union with Christ. The law itself is holy and good, but when righteousness is pursued in the flesh, even obedience becomes a form of bondage. Paul's description of inner conflict reflects life under the law without the Spirit—a condition exemplified by Saul of Tarsus. The law reveals sin and convicts the heart, but it cannot deliver. That deliverance comes only through Jesus Christ, preparing the way for the Spirit-empowered life described in Romans 8.

Application

1. Do not confuse discipline with devotion.

   Outward obedience without inward surrender cannot please God.

2. Let the law expose you, not secure you.

   Its purpose is conviction, not confidence.

3. Refuse righteousness built on obligation.

   What you do merely because you "must" will never become worship.

4. Stop asking what to do before asking who will deliver.

   Self-effort delays surrender.

5. Run from law-confidence to Christ-confidence.

   Only Christ delivers from the body of death.

Prayer

Father,

We thank You for Your holy law, which reveals truth and exposes sin. We confess that in our flesh we cannot submit to You, nor obey for the right reasons. Deliver us from confidence in obligation and from righteousness built on self-effort. Bring us, like Paul, to the end of ourselves, that we may rest wholly in Jesus Christ our Lord. Prepare our hearts for the life of the Spirit, and teach us to serve You in newness of life, not in the oldness of the letter.

We pray to You,

in the name of Jesus Christ. Amen.

Fortress of Justification

18

Life Inside the Fortress

I f Romans 7 exposes the futility of law-keeping in the flesh, Romans 8 announces the triumph of life in the Spirit. The cry of the previous chapter—"O wretched man that I am! who shall deliver me?"—is answered immediately and decisively:

> *"There is therefore now no condemnation to them which are in Christ Jesus." (Romans 8:1)*

Romans 8 does not describe a higher class of Christian or an optional spiritual experience. It describes the normal life of those who have been justified by God. Paul now unfolds the benefits of justification, not as abstract theology, but as lived reality: a new standing, a new Spirit, a new obligation, and a new inheritance.

This is life inside the fortress—not merely protected from judgment, but animated by God Himself.

No Condemnation: A New Standing

"There is therefore now no condemnation to them which are in Christ Jesus." (Romans 8:1)

Paul does not say there is less condemnation, or delayed condemnation, or suspended condemnation. He says no condemnation.

This does not mean the believer is innocent. Scripture is clear that all have sinned. What has changed is not the record of guilt, but the verdict. That guilt has been fully propitiated by the blood of Christ. The believer stands before God uncondemned.

Condemnation is not removed by improved behavior. Jesus Himself said, "He that believeth on him is not condemned: but he that believeth not is condemned already" (John 3:18). Humanity does not move into condemnation by sinning; humanity begins there. The only escape is union with Christ.

And once God, the Judge of all the earth, has declared a person justified, there is no higher court of appeal. Satan may accuse—his very name means "accuser"—but every charge is answered by the blood of Christ. God's verdict is final.

This is the first great benefit of justification: a settled standing before God.

A New Spirit: Life Where the Law Failed

"For the law of the Spirit of life in Christ Jesus hath made me free from the law of sin and death." (Romans 8:2)

The law could diagnose sin, but it could not cure it. Its weakness was not in itself, but "through the flesh" (v. 3). God accomplished what the law could not by sending His Son, condemning sin in the flesh, and establishing a new principle of life: the Spirit of life in Christ Jesus.

Paul now introduces the controlling contrast of the chapter: flesh and Spirit.

"They that are after the flesh do mind the things of the flesh; but they that are after the Spirit the things of the Spirit." (Romans 8:5)

This is not a contrast between physical and non-physical existence, but between two governing powers. The flesh is fallen human nature operating independently of God. The Spirit is the divine life given to the believer.

The mind set on the flesh is death—not merely future death, but present alienation from God—because "the carnal mind is enmity against God" and "is not subject to the law of God, neither indeed can be" (vv. 7–8). The flesh cannot submit; therefore it cannot please God.

But Paul makes a decisive declaration:

> "Ye are not in the flesh, but in the Spirit, if so be that the Spirit of God dwell in you." (Romans 5:9)

Every true believer has the Spirit of God. This is not a later experience or a second blessing. If a person does not have the Spirit of Christ, Paul says plainly, "he is none of his."

The same Spirit who raised Jesus from the dead now dwells in the believer. That Spirit gives life now—enabling righteous living even in mortal bodies—and promises resurrection later. These bodies, though still subject to weakness and decay, are already being claimed for eternal purposes.

Justification does not leave the believer unchanged. God does not merely forgive; He indwells.

A New Obligation: Living as Sons

"Therefore, brethren, we are debtors..."

Grace does not eliminate obligation; it redefines it.

The believer is no longer obligated to the flesh. That debt has been paid in full by Christ. To live according to the flesh is to live as though redemption never occurred—and that path leads only to death.

Instead, the believer is obligated to live by the Spirit:

> *"If ye through the Spirit do mortify the deeds of the body, ye shall live." (Romans 8:13)*

This is not legalism. It is not earning favor. It is the proper response of new life. Those who are "led by the Spirit of God" are not slaves driven by fear, but sons walking in obedience.

Grace does not produce passivity. It produces Spirit-empowered responsibility.

A New Relationship: The Spirit of Adoption

> *"For ye have not received the spirit of bondage again to fear; but ye have received the Spirit of adoption, whereby we cry, Abba, Father." (Romans 8:15)*

This is the first time in Romans that Paul explicitly speaks of sonship. God has not merely freed slaves; He has adopted children.

The Roman world understood adoption as a legal act that granted full status as an heir. Former slaves, once freed, were often adopted into families so they would have a name, a future, and protection. Adoption was not sentimental—it was decisive.

So it is with salvation. God did not rescue us and leave us to fend for ourselves. He brought us into His household, gave us His name, and granted us full standing as sons.

The Spirit Himself bears witness with our spirit that we are children of God. This relationship is not distant or formal. "*Abba*" is the language of intimacy—the cry of a child who belongs.

Justification does not merely settle accounts. It creates family.

A New Inheritance: Suffering and Glory

"And if children, then heirs; heirs of God, and joint-heirs with Christ..." (Romans 8:17)

The believer's future is bound to Christ's future. What He inherits, we inherit with Him. This includes glory—but it also includes suffering.

> *"If so be that we suffer with him, that we may be also glorified together." (Romans 8:17)*

Sonship carries privilege, but it also carries responsibility. Before inheritance comes labor. Before glory comes faithfulness. The believer is called to serve the Father's estate now, trusting that what is promised will be revealed in due time.

Suffering does not negate sonship; it confirms it. To bear Christ's name in a hostile world, to obey when it is costly, to endure when it is inconvenient—these are not signs of abandonment, but of belonging.

The inheritance is certain. The path includes hardship. The end is glory.

Summary

Romans 8:1–17 unfolds the blessings of justification. Those who are in Christ stand under no condemnation, possess the indwelling Spirit of God, and live under a new obligation shaped by sonship rather than fear. The Spirit gives present power for righteous living and guarantees future resurrection. Believers are adopted into God's family as heirs, sharing both the sufferings and the coming glory of Christ. Justification does not merely rescue from judgment; it establishes a new life, a new relationship, and an eternal inheritance.

Application

1. Rest in God's verdict.

    No accusation can overturn what God has declared.

2. Live by the Spirit you have received.

    You are not waiting for more power; you are called to rely on the power already given.

3. Reject fleshly autopilot.

    Life lived without reference to eternity is life lived beneath your calling.

4. Embrace your obligation as a son.

    Service is not a burden—it is preparation for inheritance.

5. Do not fear suffering.

    It is not a sign of loss, but a pathway to shared glory with Christ.

Prayer

Father,

We thank You that in Christ there is no condemnation. Thank You for giving us not only forgiveness, but Your own Spirit, dwelling within us. Teach us to live as sons, not as slaves—to walk by the Spirit and not according to the flesh. Shape our hearts toward eternity, strengthen us in suffering, and prepare us for the inheritance You have promised. May our lives display the glory of Your grace, as we serve You with joy and confidence. We pray to You,

in the name of Jesus Christ. Amen.

Fortress of Justification

19

Stamped for Glory

Romans 8 has been unfolding the benefits of justification: no condemnation, the indwelling Spirit, adoption, obligation, and inheritance. But Paul has also said something that can sound unsettling:

> *"If so be that we suffer with him, that we may be also glorified together." (Romans 8:17)*

That sentence teaches two truths at once. First, suffering belongs to the Christian life. Second, suffering is not wasted. It is not random, and it is not permanent.

Romans 8:18–30 is Paul's argument that the pain of this present time has a purpose, and that purpose is tied to a glory that will not only be revealed to us, but revealed in us.

The Weight of Glory Outweighs the Weight of Suffering

"For I reckon that the sufferings of this present time are not worthy to be compared with the glory which shall be revealed in us." (Romans 8:18)

Paul does not deny suffering. He does not minimize it. He does not rebuke the believer for feeling its weight. He acknowledges it plainly: there are "sufferings of this present time."

But he insists they are not comparable to what is coming—not because suffering is small, but because glory is overwhelming.

Suffering also has something else that gives courage to endure: it has an expiration date. It will end. And it will end well.

There are pains we can bear precisely because we know they will not last forever. Endless discomfort is crushing; but a trial with an end, even a severe one, can be endured. Paul is anchoring the believer in that kind of endurance: suffering is real, but it is not final.

Creation Groans Because Creation Was Subjugated

Paul widens the lens. The Christian's groaning is not isolated. It is part of a cosmic condition.

"For the earnest expectation of the creature waiteth for the manifestation of the sons of God." (Romans 8:19)

Creation itself is pictured as waiting—leaning forward, watching, longing. Why?

"For the creature was made subject to vanity, not willingly, but by reason of him who hath subjected the same in hope." (Romans 8:20)

Creation did not choose decay. It was subjected to futility. The world is not as it was meant to be. The bondage of corruption is not merely "how things are." It is a wound in the created order.

Yet even this subjection was not without hope:

"Because the creature itself also shall be delivered from the bondage of corruption into the glorious liberty of the children of God." (Romans 8:21)

Creation's future is tied to the sons of God. When God completes His work in His people, the created order will be freed as well. Until then:

"For we know that the whole creation groaneth and travaileth in pain together until now." (Romans 8:22)

The world groans because it is broken. And its groaning is not meaningless—it is labor, travail, the pain of something waiting to be made new.

We Groan Too—Because We Are Not Finished Yet

"And not only they, but ourselves also, which have the firstfruits of the Spirit, even we ourselves groan within ourselves..." (Romans 8:23)

The believer possesses "the firstfruits of the Spirit"—real, present, indwelling life. Yet even with the Spirit, we groan. Why?

Because adoption has begun but not yet reached its final visible form:

"...waiting for the adoption, to wit, the redemption of our body." (v. 23)

Paul calls us sons; he also says we wait for adoption. There is no contradiction. We possess sonship legally and truly now, but its full display—resurrection, transformation, glory—is still ahead.

This is why hope is essential:

"For we are saved by hope: but hope that is seen is not hope..." (Romans 8:24)

Biblical hope is not wishful thinking. It is certainty about what God has promised, combined with patience for God's timing. We do not hope for what we already possess. We hope for what is guaranteed but not yet seen.

Therefore, we "wait for it with patience" (v. 25). The Christian life is lived forward.

The Spirit Helps When We Do Not Know How to Pray

Suffering does more than hurt; it weakens.

"Likewise the Spirit also helpeth our infirmities: for we know not what we should pray for as we ought..." (Romans 8:26)

There are seasons when the believer knows what is right but cannot find words. There are burdens too heavy to articulate. Paul does not shame the believer for that weakness; he points to the Spirit's ministry:

"...the Spirit itself maketh intercession for us with groanings which cannot be uttered." (Romans 8:26)

The Spirit does not merely observe the believer's suffering; He carries it into the presence of God.

"And he that searcheth the hearts knoweth what is the mind of the Spirit..." (Romans 8:27)

The Father understands the Spirit's intercession perfectly, because the Spirit intercedes "according to the will of God." The believer is not left alone in suffering—not even in prayer.

All Things Work Together for Good

"And we know that all things work together for good to them that love God, to them who are the called according to his purpose." (Romans 8:28)

This verse is often spoken quickly and applied shallowly. A person suffering is told, "All things work together for good," as though the statement itself is meant to remove pain. It does not. Pain is not undone by slogans.

But the verse is true. The question is: what does Paul mean by "good"?

Good is not the same as pleasant. Good is not the same as comfortable. Good does not mean God arranges life so that nothing hard happens. The "good" in view is the good of God's purpose.

Sometimes what is "good" is like a surgeon cutting away rot. It may hurt. It may feel severe. But it is good because it removes what is destroying life and produces health.

This promise is also not a vague proverb for anyone who says, "Everything happens for a reason." Paul is describing a specific people: "them that love God... the called according to his purpose." He is speaking of those who belong to Christ, those who are being carried along God's saving design.

And then Paul explains what that purpose is.

Predestined for Conformity

"For whom he did foreknow, he also did predestinate to be conformed to the image of his Son..." (Romans 8:29)

Paul does not say God predestined certain people to be saved while refusing others. That is not the question he is answering here. His point is different: God's purpose for those who are His is conformity to Christ.

God foreknows His people. Nothing surprises Him. He stands outside time; He sees the whole course of history. And those whom He knows as His, He places on a path—He predestines them—for a particular end:

"to be conformed to the image of his Son."

This is not an abstract doctrine meant to stir arguments. It is a pastoral doctrine meant to stabilize sufferers. If God has set your destination, then the road is not random.

Paul's word "image" is the word eikōn—image, likeness—the same concept Christ invoked when He held up a coin and asked, "Whose image and superscription is this?" (Matthew 22:20). Caesar's image on the coin signified Caesar's claim. That coin circulated under his authority.

Paul's point is that the believer is being marked, shaped, impressed—so that Christ's image is displayed upon the believer's life. We go into the world not under our own authority, but under the authority of our King, bearing His likeness.

The Striking of the Coin

The process by which a coin bears an image is not gentle. It is not painted on. It is stamped—struck—impressed.

A blank is melted, formed, shaped, and then brought under the press. The image is struck into it. Heat, pressure, cutting, loss—everything in the process changes the metal from what it was into what it must become.

So it is with the believer. The world's image once pressed us into its mold. But God has claimed us for another likeness. He does not simply advise us to improve. He works in us—sometimes through pressure and pain—to stamp the image of His Son upon our lives.

That is why suffering is not meaningless for the Christian. It is often part of the striking.

And it explains Paul's earlier statement:

"For I reckon that the sufferings of this present time are not worthy to be compared with the glory which shall be revealed in us." (Romans 8:18)

The glory is not only future resurrection glory—though that will be beyond words. The glory is also this: Christ being displayed in His people. Christ revealed in us as His image becomes visible, tested, and proven.

Even Christ's own glory was revealed most vividly at the cross. The resurrection confirmed that glory, but the cross displayed it. Likewise, God is not only preparing a future body; He is forming a present witness.

The Golden Chain: God Finishes What He Starts

"Moreover whom he did predestinate, them he also called: and whom he called, them he also justified: and whom he justified, them he also glorified." (Romans 8:30)

Paul speaks of glory in the past tense—"glorified"—because God's purpose is settled. The chain is unbroken. The God who foreknows, predestinates, calls, and justifies does not abandon His work halfway.

This is the comfort of the believer in suffering: if God has begun the work, He will finish it. The process may involve heat and pressure. But the end is certain: conformity to Christ and glory with Christ.

Summary

Romans 8:18–30 teaches that present suffering is real but temporary, and it serves a purpose tied to future and present glory. Creation groans under the bondage of corruption, waiting for the revealing of the sons of God. Believers also groan, having the firstfruits of the Spirit while awaiting the redemption of their bodies. In weakness, the Spirit intercedes according to God's will. God works all things together for good for those who love Him and are called according to His purpose

—the good of being conformed to the image of His Son. Those God foreknew He predestined for conformity, called, justified, and will certainly glorify.

Application

1. Treat suffering as temporary, not ultimate.

   The present time is not the final time.

2. Define "good" by God's purpose, not your comfort.

   God's "good" is often refining, curative, and sanctifying.

3. Expect the process to involve pressure.

   Conformity is not painted on; it is impressed.

4. When you cannot pray, do not despair.

   The Spirit intercedes when words fail.

5. Interpret your life through the end God has set.

   If God's purpose is to conform you to Christ, then nothing is wasted—not even what hurts.

Prayer

Father,

We thank You that our lives are not random and that nothing takes You by surprise. Teach us to measure present suffering by coming glory, and to define good by Your purpose rather than our comfort. When we groan and do not know how to pray, thank You for the Spirit who intercedes according to Your will. Give us discernment to repent when our pain is the fruit of our own sin, and perseverance when You are refining us for Christlikeness. Stamp the image of Your Son upon us, that our lives may display His glory to the world.

We pray to You,

in the name of Jesus Christ. Amen.

20

The
Unbroken
Bond

Romans 8 opens with an unshakable declaration:

"There is therefore now no condemnation to them which are in Christ Jesus." (Romans 8:1)

It closes with an equally unshakable persuasion:

"For I am persuaded, that neither death, nor life... nor any other creature, shall be able to separate us from the love of God, which is in Christ Jesus our Lord." (Romans 8:38-39)

Between those two statements, Paul has unfolded the full weight and wonder of justification. The believer stands acquitted. The Spirit dwells within. Adoption has been granted. Glory has been promised. Even suffering—once meaningless and destructive—has been gathered into God's redemptive purpose.

Now, as Paul brings the chapter to its close, he does not merely reassure the believer of God's love. He presses a deeper question—one that lies at the heart of covenant faithfulness.

If God Is for Us

"What shall we then say to these things? If God be for us, who can be against us?" (Romans 8:31)

Paul is not suggesting the absence of enemies. The church in Rome knew opposition well—social, religious, and increasingly political. What Paul asserts is that no opposition can overturn what God has purposed.

If God has predestined His people to be conformed to the image of His Son, no rival plan can derail that purpose. If God has called, justified, and begun the work of glorification, no accusation can undo it. The fortress does not stand because it is unchallenged; it stands because its foundation is God Himself.

The Measure of God's Gift

"He that spared not his own Son, but delivered him up for us all, how shall he not with him also freely give us all things?" (Romans 8:32)

Paul argues from the greater to the lesser. God has already given what cannot be surpassed—the Son of His love. Having given Christ, He will not withhold what is necessary to complete His work in those who belong to Him.

This promise is not of comfort without cost, nor of blessing without obedience. It is the assurance that everything God intends to give His people is bound up in Christ. There is no second inheritance, no hidden tier of blessing. With Christ comes all that God has purposed.

No Charge, No Condemnation

"Who shall lay any thing to the charge of God's elect? It is God that justifieth.

Who is he that condemneth? It is Christ that died, yea rather, that is risen again..." (Romans 8:33–34)

The language is judicial. Charges are imagined, accusers named, verdicts considered. But every attempt collapses under the same reality: God justifies.

Christ has died. Christ has risen. Christ now intercedes. The very One who could condemn has chosen instead to redeem. Condemnation cannot return without the cross being undone—and the cross will never be undone.

The Question Paul Asks

"Who shall separate us from the love of Christ? shall tribulation, or distress, or persecution, or famine, or nakedness, or peril, or sword?" *(Romans 8:35)*

This verse is often heard as a reassurance that Christ will continue loving us through suffering—and that is gloriously true. But Paul has already established that truth elsewhere, and he will state it unmistakably again in verses 38–39.

Here, however, the question is pressed from another direction.

Paul has just finished declaring that God has withheld nothing—neither His Son nor His Spirit nor His promises. He has shown that suffering itself is being used to form Christ's image in us. Now he asks: What, then, would be enough to loosen our devotion to Christ?

The pressures he lists are not abstract doubts. They are concrete trials faced precisely because one belongs to Christ. Hunger. Exposure. Danger. The sword. These are not experiences that threaten God's love; they are experiences that test our allegiance.

Faithful Suffering

"As it is written, For thy sake we are killed all the day long; we are accounted as sheep for the slaughter." (Romans 8:36)

Paul quotes Psalm 44—a psalm not of apostasy, but of bewildered faithfulness. The psalmist insists that God's people have not abandoned the covenant, even as suffering overwhelms them. The pain is real. The purpose is unclear. But loyalty remains.

This is not the language of divine abandonment. It is the language of covenant endurance.

Paul is reminding the church that suffering has always been the context in which love proves itself—not by sentiment, but by steadfastness.

More Than Conquerors

"Nay, in all these things we are more than conquerors through him that loved us."
(Romans 8:37)

Victory does not consist in avoiding suffering, but in refusing to abandon Christ within it. The believer conquers not by escaping the fire, but by remaining faithful in it—trusting that what God is forming through hardship is more valuable than what comfort would preserve.

The victory is not self-generated. It flows "through him that loved us." Christ's initiating love secures the believer even as the believer's love is tested and refined.

The Unbreakable Assurance

"For I am persuaded, that neither death, nor life... nor any other creature, shall be able to separate us from the love of God, which is in Christ Jesus our Lord." (Romans 8:38–39)

Paul now seals the argument from God's side of the covenant. Having pressed the believer to consider the cost of loyalty, he leaves no doubt about the certainty of divine love.

No state of existence—living or dying.

No spiritual power—angelic or demonic.

No dimension of space or time.

No unforeseen circumstance within creation.

Nothing can sever the believer from God's love in Christ.

The bond may be tested from the human side, but it is secured from the divine side. God's love does not waver, withdraw, or fail.

Summary

Romans 8:31–39 brings Paul's argument to its triumphant conclusion. God's saving purpose cannot be overturned, His provision cannot be exhausted, His verdict cannot be reversed, and His love cannot be broken. In the midst of suffering, Paul does not merely reassure believers that God still loves them; he calls them to steadfast, reciprocal love—loyalty that endures because it rests upon God's unchanging grace. Nothing can separate the believer from God's love, and therefore nothing is finally sufficient to justify abandoning Christ.

Application

1. Rest in God's verdict.

   Condemnation has no authority where God has justified.

2. Interpret suffering through covenant, not suspicion.

   Hardship is not evidence of abandonment, but often the means of formation.

3. Let love mature into loyalty.

   God's love for you is settled; your love for Christ is refined through faithfulness.

4. Refuse lesser allegiances.

   Nothing offered by the world is worth surrendering what Christ has given.

5. Stand persuaded.

   Assurance is not denial of pain, but confidence in God's unbreakable purpose.

Prayer

Father,

We thank You that You are for us, that You did not spare Your own Son, and that You have justified us fully in Christ. Teach us to interpret suffering through Your faithfulness rather than our fear. Strengthen our love for Christ when obedience is costly, and anchor our assurance in the truth that nothing can separate us from Your love. Form the image of Your Son in us, and make us steadfast in loyalty and hope.

We pray to You,

in the name of Jesus Christ. Amen.

Fortress of Justification

21

The Potter's Right and the Promise's Line

Romans 8 ends with a settled triumph: God will not stop loving His people, and nothing in creation can sever us from His love in Christ Jesus. But the moment Paul says that, a Jewish objection rises immediately—because it is the objection the whole book has been anticipating.

If salvation is by grace through faith—apart from the law—then what about Israel?

God made covenants with Israel. God gave Israel promises. God chose Israel. God worked through Israel for centuries. And if now the Gentiles are entering the blessings of Messiah without becoming

Jews, and if many Jews are rejecting Messiah altogether, then does that mean God's word failed?

Romans 9 is Paul's answer. And he begins, not with argument, but with anguish.

Paul's Sorrow for Israel

Paul does not begin Romans 9 as a detached theologian; he begins as a broken-hearted Israelite.

> *"I say the truth in Christ, I lie not, my conscience also bearing me witness in the Holy Ghost,*
>
> *That I have great heaviness and continual sorrow in my heart.*
>
> *For I could wish that myself were accursed from Christ for my brethren, my kinsmen according to the flesh." (Romans 9:1–3)*

This is not staged sympathy. This is covenant grief. Paul is echoing Moses—who once pleaded with God for Israel's sake, willing to be blotted out if it would rescue the people. Paul's love is not theoretical; it is costly.

And then Paul lists Israel's privileges. He is not minimizing them. He is magnifying them—and then insisting that none of them, by themselves, produce justification.

Israel's Privileges Are Real—and Insufficient To Save

"Who are Israelites; to whom pertaineth the adoption, and the glory, and the covenants, and the giving of the law, and the service of God, and the promises;

Whose are the fathers, and of whom as concerning the flesh Christ came..." (Romans 9:4–5)

Israel had adoption in the sense of national sonship— God's choosing of a people to bear His name in the world. Israel had glory—God's manifest presence among them. Israel had covenants, law, temple service, promises, patriarchs, and even the staggering honor that Messiah came "according to the flesh" through their line.

But that entire list, for all its weight, does not equal saving faith.

A man may be born into privilege and still die outside the fortress. A family tree does not become a bridge of faith. A religious heritage is not the righteousness of God.

So Paul presses the core question: *Has God's word failed?*

God's Word Has Not Failed Because "Israel" Was Never Merely Biological

> *"Not as though the word of God hath taken none effect. For they are not all Israel, which are of Israel." (Romans 9:6)*

Paul is not inventing a new God or a new standard. He is clarifying what God has always been doing: the promise moves through God's chosen line—not through mere physical descent.

And he proves it from Genesis.

- Abraham had more than one son, but the promise moved through Isaac.

- Isaac had more than one son, but the covenant line moved through Jacob.

> *"Neither, because they are the seed of Abraham, are they all children: but, In Isaac shall thy seed be called." (Romans 9:7)*

Paul's point is not, "God chooses some babies for heaven and some for hell." His point is: God chooses the line through which He will carry His redemptive purpose forward. The promise is not inherited by biology like a family heirloom; it advances by God's purpose.

Jacob and Esau: Election Is About God's Purpose, Not Human Deserving

"(For the children being not yet born, neither having done any good or evil, that the purpose of God according to election might stand, not of works, but of him that calleth;)

It was said unto her, The elder shall serve the younger." (Romans 9:11–12)

Notice the phrasing: "The elder shall serve the younger." The language is functional. It concerns role, calling, and the line of promise. Paul is establishing a principle: God's purpose stands independent of human merit.

Then Paul quotes Malachi:

"As it is written, Jacob have I loved, but Esau have I hated." (Romans 9:13)

In context, this is covenant language of choice—not a denial of God's kindness, provision, or moral governance toward Esau as a human being. The point is not that Esau was barred from mercy as a creature;

the point is that Esau was not the chosen line for the covenant mission that would bring Messiah into the world.

Israel's election was never merely "you are automatically saved." It was: "You are chosen to carry something." Or, in the language of this book: God elected Israel to serve His redemptive purpose in history.

Malachi's "Jacob have I loved, but Esau have I hated" is spoken to a post-exilic people questioning God's love, and the context is plainly national: borders, lands, rebuilding, and the LORD's covenant posture toward Edom. It is not a psychological profile of two brothers, much less a technical decree about their eternal destinies. Paul borrows Malachi's covenant language to prove that God's promise-line has always advanced by divine choice and purpose, not by mere birth order or human deserving. Esau's story warns us of the tragedy of despising holy things; the text does not require us to conclude that Esau was created for damnation. The issue is service in the promise-line, not a denial that mercy is offered to "whosoever will."

"Is there unrighteousness with God?" No—because mercy is God's prerogative

Paul anticipates the protest.

"What shall we say then? Is there unrighteousness with God? God forbid." *(Romans 9:14)*

Then he quotes God's words to Moses:

"I will have mercy on whom I will have mercy, and I will have compassion on whom I will have compassion." (Romans 9:15)

This is not God saying, "I delight to damn." This is God asserting His freedom: mercy is not owed. If mercy is owed, it is no longer mercy. If it is earned, it is no longer grace.

So Paul concludes:

"So then it is not of him that willeth, nor of him that runneth, but of God that sheweth mercy." (Romans 9:16)

The Jewish dispute underneath Romans is exactly this: "We have law. We have covenants. We have ancestry. We have temple worship. We have Moses." Paul's answer is: None of those can compel God. None of those can purchase justification.

The fortress is entered by faith, not by pedigree.

Pharaoh: God can display His glory even through resistance

Paul moves to Pharaoh:

"For the scripture saith unto Pharaoh, Even for this same purpose have I raised thee up, that I might shew my power in thee, and that my name might be declared throughout all the earth." (Romans 9:17)

Pharaoh becomes a public stage for God's power. He is an example that God's purpose is not fragile—no ruler, no empire, no hardened will can stop it.

"Therefore hath he mercy on whom he will have mercy, and whom he will he hardeneth." (Romans 9:18)

Paul is not excusing Pharaoh. He is humbling the objector. The complaint "Why doth he yet find fault?" is the complaint of a creature trying to put the Creator in the dock.

The Potter and the clay: God has the right to form vessels for His purpose

"Nay but, O man, who art thou that repliest against God? Shall the thing formed say to him

that formed it, Why hast thou made me thus?"
(Romans 9:20)

Paul's point is simple and sobering: God is not accountable to human standards of entitlement. The potter has rights over the clay. God forms history for His ends, and He does not ask permission from the creature.

Then comes language that is often mishandled:

"What if God, willing to shew his wrath, and to make his power known, endured with much longsuffering the vessels of wrath fitted to destruction:

And that he might make known the riches of his glory on the vessels of mercy, which he had afore prepared unto glory." (Romans 9:22–23)

Two things matter here:

1. God "endured with much longsuffering"—He is patient, not impulsive.

2. The purpose is the revelation of His glory—God's plan is not random; it is purposeful.

And then Paul lands the outcome: God is calling both Jews and Gentiles into mercy—exactly as Scripture foretold.

"Even us, whom he hath called, not of the Jews only, but also of the Gentiles." (Romans 9:24)

The "chosen people" category is not revoked; it is clarified. Israel's election had a mission in history—one that always anticipated Gentile mercy.

Why Israel stumbled: they pursued righteousness the wrong way

Paul closes with the simplest explanation in the chapter.

"What shall we say then? That the Gentiles, which followed not after righteousness, have attained to righteousness...

But Israel, which followed after the law of righteousness, hath not attained...

Wherefore? Because they sought it not by faith, but as it were by the works of the law." (Romans 9:30–32)

This is the burden of Romans in one paragraph: righteousness comes by faith, not by performance.

Then the final image:

"Behold, I lay in Sion a stumblingstone and rock of offence: and whosoever believeth on him shall not be ashamed." (Romans 9:33)

Christ is the Stone. Israel stumbled not because the Stone was evil, but because self-righteousness refuses to bow. The Stone is mercy—God interrupting the headlong run of religious pride and placing Christ in the path so that sinners might be brought down low enough to believe.

Summary

Romans 9 answers the charge that God's word has failed by showing that God has always advanced His promise by His own sovereign purpose—not by human lineage, merit, or law-keeping. Israel's election was real, honored, and historically purposeful, but it was never a guarantee of personal salvation. God's mercy remains mercy, not wages; His purpose stands even against resistance; and the decisive issue is faith in Christ, the Stumbling Stone—upon whom the believer will never be ashamed.

Application

1. Do not confuse privilege with salvation.

   Heritage, knowledge, and service are blessings— but none can replace faith in Christ.

2. Receive mercy as mercy.

   Gratitude grows when you stop treating grace as something God owed you.

3. Yield to God's shaping work.

   Do not argue with the Potter. Become pliable clay —humble, teachable, obedient.

4. Let Christ trip your pride before it ruins you.

   If you have been offended by the gospel, do not curse the Stone—bow to Him.

5. Measure "election" by purpose, not entitlement.

   God calls people and nations into roles that serve His glory. The safest posture is surrender.

Prayer

Father,

You are the Sovereign God, and Your word has not failed. Forgive us for thinking You owe us mercy, as though grace were wages. Make our hearts soft and pliable in Your hands. Keep us from trusting in heritage, religious effort, or outward privilege, and bring us to simple, obedient faith in Jesus Christ. Where pride resists Your purposes, humble us. Where suffering shapes us, steady us. Form Christ in us, and let our lives display Your glory.

We pray to You,

in the name of Jesus. Amen.

Fortress of Justification

22

"Righteousness Near at Hand"

Romans 10 is one of the clearest chapters in Scripture on the simplicity of saving faith—and one of the most searching chapters on the danger of religious self-confidence. But to read it well, we must keep it where Paul placed it: inside the argument of Romans 9–11.

The presenting question in these chapters is not, "How can Gentiles be saved?" Paul has already answered that. The pressing question is, "If God made promises to Israel, and Israel has largely rejected Christ, has the Word of God failed?" Paul's answer is firm: God has not failed; Israel's stumble is real; Gentile inclusion is real; and God is still faithful to Israel. Romans 10 sits in the middle of that argument and shows us why Israel stumbled, how salvation truly comes, and why preaching is not optional.

Paul's Heart: Truth Without Coldness (Romans 10:1)

Paul opens Romans 10 with a sentence that sets the tone for everything that follows:

> *"Brethren, my heart's desire and prayer to God for Israel is, that they might be saved." (Romans 10:1)*

Paul is not arguing like a man who wants to win a debate. He is arguing like a man who wants to win his brothers. He is not speaking about Israel as an abstraction. He is speaking about his people with grief, longing, and intercession.

That matters for you as a Christian, because it is possible to be doctrinally correct and spiritually un-Christlike. Paul's posture refuses that combination. He tells the truth plainly, but he speaks it with tears. Before Paul explains Israel's error, he demonstrates the love that ought to accompany our explanations.

The Tragedy: Zeal Without Knowledge

Paul immediately acknowledges something important:

> *"For I bear them record that they have a zeal of God, but not according to knowledge."* *(Romans 10:2)*

Israel was not spiritually lazy. Their problem was not indifference. Their problem was misdirected devotion —religious energy detached from saving truth. A person can be sincere, disciplined, moral, faithful to tradition, and earnest in worship—and still be lost.

Then Paul names the heart of the issue:

> *"For they being ignorant of God's righteousness, and going about to establish their own righteousness, have not submitted themselves unto the righteousness of God."* *(Romans 10:3)*

Here is the tragedy of religious self-righteousness: it is not merely a mistake; it is a refusal. Paul says they "have not submitted." That is strong language. The problem is not simply that Israel lacked information; the problem is that Israel resisted God's righteousness because they preferred their own.

This verse exposes a pattern that appears in every human heart. We do not naturally want a righteousness that must be received. We naturally want a righteousness that can be achieved—something we can own, display, defend, and compare

Self-righteousness offers a counterfeit security: "I have done enough." God's righteousness demands a humbling surrender: "Christ is enough."

The Turning Point: Christ the End of the Law

Paul's next sentence is famous and often mishandled:

"For Christ is the end of the law for righteousness to every one that believeth." (Romans 10:4)

The word "end" here is not best taken as a casual dismissal of God's law, as though Paul were saying the law is worthless. Paul has already defended the goodness of the law (Romans 7). The point is not that the law was a mistake. The point is that the law had a purpose—and that purpose reaches its goal in Christ.

Christ is the end of the law "for righteousness." That phrase matters. Paul is not teaching that believers now despise God's moral will. He is teaching that the law was never given as a ladder by which sinners climb up into right standing with God. The law shows God's righteousness, names our unrighteousness, and drives us to the only place righteousness can be found: Christ.

So when Paul says Christ is the end of the law "for righteousness," he is saying:

- The law cannot produce a justified standing for sinners.

- Christ fulfills what the law pointed toward.

- Righteousness is now located in Christ and received by faith.

He also adds a phrase that levels every barrier:

"to every one that believeth." (Romans 10:4)

The doorway into righteousness is not ethnicity. Not moral achievement. Not religious pedigree. Not ceremonial precision. Not spiritual reputation. The doorway is faith—faith in Christ.

Two Kinds of Righteousness: Doing vs. Trusting

Paul now contrasts the righteousness that tries to live by doing with the righteousness that lives by believing.

First:

"For Moses describeth the righteousness which is of the law, That the man which doeth those things shall live by them." (Romans 10:5)

This is the unavoidable logic of law-righteousness: if you choose the law as your basis for acceptance, you must keep it—completely, continually, without defect. This is not merely demanding; it is condemning, because sinners do not keep it.

Then Paul turns:

"But the righteousness which is of faith speaketh on this wise..." (Romans 10:6)

Notice the language: righteousness "speaks." Paul is personifying faith-righteousness as a voice calling to us. What does it say?

"Say not in thine heart, Who shall ascend into heaven? (that is, to bring Christ down from above:)

Or, Who shall descend into the deep? (that is, to bring up Christ again from the dead.)" (Romans 10:6–7)

Paul's meaning is not complicated, but it is profound. He is saying: saving righteousness is not hidden behind an impossible spiritual achievement.

You do not need a heroic ascent—someone so spiritually superior that he can climb into heaven and bring Christ down. Christ has already come.

You do not need a heroic descent—someone so sacrificial that he can enter death and bring salvation back. Christ has already died and risen.

In other words: do not treat salvation as though it depends upon human capability, human mediation, or human achievement. God has acted. Christ has come. Christ has died. Christ has risen. Salvation does not wait for you to accomplish what only the Son of God could accomplish.

Then Paul brings it home:

> "But what saith it? The word is nigh thee, even in thy mouth, and in thy heart: that is, the word of faith, which we preach." (Romans 10:8)

Here is one of the great mercies of God: He puts saving truth near.

Not near as a vague sentiment. Not near as a mystical feeling. Near as a message—the word of faith, which we preach.

Paul is drawing from Deuteronomy 30, where Moses told Israel that God's word was not inaccessible—no need to cross the sea, no need to ascend into heaven. Paul takes that principle and shows its fulfillment in the gospel: the saving word is near because God has brought it near through Christ and through preaching.

The Great Confession: The Mouth and the Heart

Paul now states the gospel in a form so direct that generations have memorized it:

> *"That if thou shalt confess with thy mouth the Lord Jesus, and shalt believe in thine heart that God hath raised him from the dead, thou shalt be saved." (Romans 10:9)*

We must not shrink this into a formula, as if salvation were a mere recitation. Paul is describing the outward and inward expressions of genuine faith:

• Confession with the mouth: Jesus is Lord.

• Belief in the heart: God raised Him from the dead.

This is not "faith in faith." It is not vague optimism. It is not mere agreement with religious ideas. It is a personal, heart-level resting in Christ—and a public acknowledgment that Jesus has rightful authority.

Paul continues:

"For with the heart man believeth unto righteousness; and with the mouth confession is made unto salvation." (Romans 10:10)

Believing "unto righteousness" means faith unites the sinner to Christ, so that what Christ is and what Christ has done becomes the believer's standing before God. Confession "unto salvation" means that true faith does not remain a private preference. It yields allegiance.

This does not turn salvation into works. It shows what faith is. Faith is not merely receiving Christ as a helper; it is receiving Christ as Lord. A man cannot cling to his own throne and call Jesus Lord at the same time. Faith dethrones self.

The Universal Promise: No Distinction

Paul now supports his gospel claims with Scripture:

"For the scripture saith, Whosoever believeth on him shall not be ashamed." (Romans 10:11)

Then he states one of the great equalizers of the New Testament:

"For there is no difference between the Jew and the Greek: for the same Lord over all is

rich unto all that call upon him." (Romans 10:12)

The dividing wall that human pride loves to build— ethnic, cultural, moral, religious—cannot stand at the foot of the cross. There is one Lord. And He is "rich unto all" who call upon Him.

Then Paul seals it:

"For whosoever shall call upon the name of the Lord shall be saved." (Romans 10:13)

This "whosoever" is not weak. It is strong. It is the open door of God's mercy.

But notice what "call upon the name of the Lord" implies. To call upon His name is not merely to ask for assistance while keeping control. In Scripture, the "name" represents the person—His authority, His character, His rightful claim. Calling on His name is a cry of dependence and submission: "Lord, I cannot save myself. I am yours. Save me."

So Paul is not saying that a man is saved by a moment of emotional intensity. He is saying that salvation comes to the one who truly calls on the Lord —trusting Him and yielding to Him.

Why Preaching Is Essential

Now Paul turns toward the necessary means God uses to bring that "whosoever" to actual faith:

"How then shall they call on him in whom they have not believed? and how shall they believe in him of whom they have not heard? and how shall they hear without a preacher?" (Romans 10:14)

Paul's chain is relentless:

- No calling without believing.

- No believing without hearing.

- No hearing without preaching.

Then:

"And how shall they preach, except they be sent?" (Romans 10:15)

Preaching is not a hobby. It is a commission. God sends heralds with a message.

Paul then quotes:

"How beautiful are the feet of them that preach the gospel of peace, and bring glad tidings of good things!" (Romans 10:15)

Why "beautiful feet"? Because they arrive with news that changes everything: peace with God through Christ.

Paul immediately adds a sober qualifier:

"But they have not all obeyed the gospel." *(Romans 10:16)*

Hearing does not automatically produce obedience. The gospel is not merely information; it is a summons. Some obey; some refuse.

Then Paul quotes Isaiah:

"Lord, who hath believed our report?" (Romans 10:16)

Isaiah knew what it was to proclaim truth and be rejected. Paul draws that connection because the Jewish rejection of Christ is not a strange accident; it is a pattern Israel's prophets experienced again and again.

Then Paul gives a statement that governs the entire Christian understanding of conversion:

"So then faith cometh by hearing, and hearing by the word of God." (Romans 10:17)

Faith does not come by argument alone. Not by pressure. Not by entertainment. Not by cultural inheritance. Faith comes by hearing—and hearing by the Word of God.

This is why the preaching of Scripture cannot be replaced by merely sharing opinions about Scripture. The Word itself is God's instrument. God creates faith by the gospel announcement of Christ.

Israel's Responsibility and God's Long Patience

Paul anticipates an objection: "But perhaps Israel did not hear?"

"But I say, Have they not heard? Yes verily..."
(Romans 10:18)

Paul's point is not that every Israelite had equal exposure to every messenger, but that Israel, as a people, had received light—Scripture, prophets, promises, the public ministry of Christ, apostolic witness. The problem was not absence of light but resistance to it.

Then Paul asks another question: "But perhaps Israel did not understand?"

"But I say, Did not Israel know?" (Romans 10:19)

And Paul answers by quoting Moses and Isaiah: God foretold that Gentiles—those who were "not a nation" in covenantal terms—would be brought in, and that this would provoke Israel to jealousy. The point is not mere provocation; it is mercy. God uses Gentile inclusion as a means to awaken Israel.

Finally Paul quotes a devastating line from Isaiah:

> *"All day long I have stretched forth my hands unto a disobedient and gainsaying people."* *(Romans 10:21)*

Here is God's posture toward Israel: hands stretched out "all day long." That is not the picture of a reluctant God. That is not the picture of a cruel God. That is the picture of a God who calls, invites, pleads, and persists—while a stubborn people refuse.

Romans 10 therefore holds two truths together:

1. Israel is responsible for rejecting God's righteousness in Christ.

2. God is still patient, still purposeful, still faithful— and still stretching out His hands.

This is exactly where Romans 9–11 is heading: Israel's present state is not the end of the story. But Romans 10 insists that Israel's present refusal is real refusal—rooted in prideful self-righteousness, not in a lack of available truth.

Summary

Romans 10 teaches that Israel's great problem was not lack of zeal but self-righteous zeal—a refusal to submit to God's righteousness in Christ. The law could describe righteousness, but it could not produce righteousness. Christ is the law's end "for righteousness," meaning He is the fulfillment and goal where righteousness is found and received by faith.

Saving righteousness is not distant or inaccessible. God has brought it near through the preached Word. The gospel is received by believing in the heart and confessed by acknowledging Jesus as Lord. This salvation is open to all: "whosoever" calls on the Lord will be saved, with no distinction between Jew and Gentile.

Because faith comes by hearing, preaching is essential. Yet not all obey the gospel; Israel's rejection is a real moral refusal, not a mere misunderstanding. And still God's posture toward Israel is patient mercy —hands stretched out "all day long."

Application

1. Do not trust religious effort as though it were submission

   You can be zealous and still be lost. Religious activity becomes deadly when it becomes self-justification. Ask plainly: am I obeying as a redeemed son, or performing as a self-righteous laborer?

2. **Receive God's righteousness instead of negotiating for your own**

Romans 10 calls you to stop "going about" establishing your own righteousness. The gospel does not improve your résumé; it ends your boasting. Come empty-handed to Christ.

3. **Treat confession as allegiance, not a slogan**

To confess "Jesus is Lord" is not merely to say words; it is to agree with reality and surrender to it. This confession will reshape priorities, decisions, and loyalties—not to earn salvation, but because salvation has changed ownership.

4. **Keep preaching central—especially to those you love**

Faith comes by hearing the Word of God. If you want sinners to be saved, you must bring them to Christ through Scripture—patiently, clearly, repeatedly. Do not substitute spiritual talk for gospel proclamation.

5. **Learn God's posture: stretched-out hands**

When you meet stubbornness—whether in Israel, in your family, or in your own heart—remember

God's posture in Romans 10: hands stretched out all day long. Let that shape your evangelism and your patience.

Prayer

Father,

We come to You thankful that Your righteousness is not a prize for the strong, but a gift for the humble. By Your Spirit, expose every place where we are still trying to establish our own righteousness—every place where pride has disguised itself as zeal. Bring us to real submission, where we stop resisting and rest our whole confidence in Christ.

We confess that Jesus is Lord. Teach us what that confession means in daily life: surrendered priorities, obedient choices, faithful endurance, and steady hope. Make Your Word living and near to us, not merely familiar. And make us people who speak it— clearly, lovingly, and without fear—so that faith may come by hearing.

We pray for Israel, as Paul did: that they would be saved, that they would see Christ as the righteousness of God, and that Your stretched-out hands would draw many to repentance and faith. Keep us from hardness of heart, and keep us from the deadly comfort of self-righteous religion.

We ask all of this to the Father,

in the name of Jesus. Amen.

23

The Root
Supports
the Branches

Romans 11 completes Paul's three-chapter answer (Romans 9–11) to a question that would not go away in the Roman church: Has God failed Israel? If the Gentiles are now coming to Christ in great numbers, and the Jews are largely rejecting Him, does that mean God has rejected Israel and replaced her with the church?

Paul's answer is emphatic: *absolutely not*. Israel's present condition is real and serious—but it is not final, and it is not proof that God's promises have collapsed. In Romans 11, Paul shows (1) that God has preserved a remnant, (2) that Israel's stumble has served a saving purpose for the nations, (3) that

Gentile believers must fear pride and guard against presumption, and (4) that God will yet act in mercy toward Israel in a future restoration.

The First Answer: God Has Not Rejected His People

Paul begins with a direct question:

> "I say then, Hath God cast away his people? God forbid." (Romans 11:1)

That "God forbid" is as strong as Paul knows how to be. It is not a gentle correction. It is a refusal. The idea that God has discarded Israel as a people is incompatible with God's character and covenant faithfulness.

Paul immediately offers his first evidence:

> "For I also am an Israelite, of the seed of Abraham, of the tribe of Benjamin." (Romans 11:1)

Paul is not speaking theoretically. He is living proof that Jews can and do come to Christ, and that Jewish identity is not an automatic barrier to salvation. The existence of Jewish believers—then and now—stands against the claim that God has rejected Israel in total.

Then Paul expands the argument:

"God hath not cast away his people which he foreknew." (Romans 11:2)

"Foreknew" here is covenant language. Paul is not claiming that Israel is saved by ethnicity. He is claiming that God has a covenantal relationship with this people in history—real promises, real commitments, real intentions still unfolding. Israel's unbelief does not unmake God's faithfulness.

Elijah and the Remnant

Paul then reaches back to Elijah:

"Lord, they have killed thy prophets... and I am left alone, and they seek my life." (Romans 11:3)

"But what saith the answer of God unto him? I have reserved to myself seven thousand men..." (Romans 11:4)

Elijah looked at national apostasy and assumed total collapse. God corrected him: there was a faithful remnant Elijah could not see. Paul's point is crucial: the existence of a remnant is not a new idea; it is the consistent pattern in Israel's history.

So Paul concludes:

"Even so then at this present time also there is a remnant according to the election of grace." *(Romans 11:5)*

The remnant exists "according to… grace." It is not produced by law-keeping, ancestry, or ceremonial identity. It exists because God shows mercy and creates faith.

And Paul tightens it with a line that cannot be softened:

"And if by grace, then is it no more of works… otherwise grace is no more grace." *(Romans 11:6)*

Paul is not allowing anyone—Jew or Gentile—to smuggle human merit into the foundation of salvation. If salvation is grace, it is grace. If it is works, it is works. You cannot blend the two as though God were partially Savior and you were partially savior.

The Second Answer: Israel's Hardening Is Real, but Not Ultimate

Paul states what has happened:

"Israel hath not obtained that which he seeketh for; but the election hath obtained it, and the rest were blinded." *(Romans 11:7)*

Israel sought righteousness, but sought it the wrong way—by works, by self-establishment, by refusing submission to God's righteousness in Christ (Romans 10:3). A remnant "obtained it" because they obtained Christ by faith.

Then Paul describes the condition of "the rest" as blinding/hardening and supports it from Scripture. The doctrinal point here must be handled carefully, because Paul is not denying Israel's responsibility. The broader argument in Romans 10 insists that Israel is culpable for resisting light. Romans 11 is describing God's judicial action in response to persistent rejection—God giving people over to what they have insisted upon.

Paul adds the sobering imagery of Psalm 69:

> "Let their table be made a snare..." (Romans 11:9)

A "table" is a place of provision, abundance, satisfaction. The tragedy is not merely that Israel lacked blessings; the tragedy is that blessings— misread and misused—became a trap. When the gifts of God become substitutes for God, they harden rather than heal.

This is one of the most urgent warnings in the chapter, and it is aimed especially at people who have had much exposure to truth. Familiarity can become dangerous if it produces contempt, complacency, or spiritual sleep.

The Third Answer: Israel's Stumble Served the Gentiles—and Is Meant to Provoke Israel

Paul asks another question:

"Have they stumbled that they should fall? God forbid." (Romans 11:11)

Israel's stumble is not an irrevocable plunge into permanent ruin. God has a purpose in it.

"But rather through their fall salvation is come unto the Gentiles, for to provoke them to jealousy." (Romans 11:11)

This is not petty jealousy. It is redemptive provocation: Israel is meant to see Gentiles enjoying Israel's Messiah, Israel's Scriptures, Israel's covenant blessings fulfilled in Christ—and to be awakened to what they have refused.

Paul then argues from the lesser to the greater:

"If the fall of them be the riches of the world... how much more their fulness?" (Romans 11:12)

If Gentile salvation has come through Israel's rejection, what will happen when God acts in mercy to bring Israel back? Paul's language becomes almost resurrection-like:

> "What shall the receiving of them be, but life from the dead?" (Romans 11:15)

Paul is describing a future work of God so dramatic that it will feel like a great awakening—an event that shakes history and magnifies mercy.

The Olive Tree: A Warning to Gentile Pride

Paul now turns directly to the Gentile believers, and this is where the chapter presses on the conscience.

He uses an olive tree image. The root is holy; the branches belong to it; some natural branches have been broken off; and Gentiles—like a wild olive shoot —have been grafted in.

Then Paul delivers the sentence Gentile believers most need to hear:

> "Boast not against the branches... Thou bearest not the root, but the root thee." (Romans 11:18, KJV)

The Gentile Christian does not replace Israel as though Israel were merely disposable. Gentiles are included by mercy into a story they did not originate. The root—covenant revelation, promises, Scriptures, Messiah according to the flesh—came through Israel. The Gentile believer is not the foundation; he is the beneficiary.

Paul anticipates the proud Gentile response:

> *"The branches were broken off, that I might be grafted in." (Romans 11:19)*

Paul replies:

> *"Well; because of unbelief they were broken off, and thou standest by faith. Be not highminded, but fear." (Romans 11:20)*

This is not fear of losing Christ as though salvation were fragile. It is fear of presumption—the fear that comes from taking mercy for granted and turning grace into entitlement.

Then Paul says something that should sober every church:

> *"For if God spared not the natural branches, take heed lest he also spare not thee." (Romans 11:21)*

The warning is not that God is fickle. The warning is that God does not tolerate unbelief dressed in religious clothing. If Israel had the Scriptures, the rituals, the temple worship, and still stumbled through unbelief, then Gentiles must not assume that having Christian vocabulary, Christian institutions, and Christian traditions makes them invulnerable.

Paul then commands the reader to look straight at the character of God:

> *"Behold therefore the goodness and severity of God…" (Romans 11:22)*

A God who is only "goodness" in our minds becomes a sentimental idol. A God who is only "severity" becomes a tyrant in our minds. Paul refuses both distortions. God is merciful and just; patient and holy; generous and unsparing toward hardened unbelief.

And then Paul holds out hope:

> *"And they also, if they abide not still in unbelief, shall be grafted in: for God is able to graft them in again." (Romans 11:23)*

That one line is important: God is able. The same mercy that brought Gentiles in can bring Israel back. The same power that grafted wild branches into a cultivated root can graft natural branches back into their own tree.

The Mystery: Partial Hardening Until the Fullness of the Gentiles

Paul now reveals what he calls a "mystery"—not something spooky, but something previously hidden that God now discloses:

"Blindness in part is happened to Israel, until the fulness of the Gentiles be come in." *(Romans 11:25)*

"Blindness in part" means two things at once:

1. Not every Jew is blind (there is a remnant).

2. Israel's blindness is not permanent (it has an "until").

Then comes Paul's climactic statement:

"And so all Israel shall be saved..." (Romans 11:26)

This is one of the most debated phrases in Romans. But in the flow of Paul's argument—Paul is describing a future, large-scale turning of Israel to Christ in connection with the Deliverer coming out of Zion and the removal of ungodliness from Jacob. Paul anchors this in prophetic Scripture and ties it to covenant mercy:

"For the gifts and calling of God are without repentance." (Romans 11:29)

Meaning: God does not revoke what He has promised simply because human beings are unfaithful. If covenant faithfulness depends on human constancy, no one survives. But if covenant faithfulness depends on God's character, then mercy can have the final word.

Paul then explains the mercy logic that has encompassed both Jew and Gentile:

• Gentiles were disobedient, then received mercy.

• Israel is now in disobedience, and mercy will yet reach them.

• God has ordered history so that no group can boast —only marvel.

  "For God hath concluded them all in unbelief, that he might have mercy upon all." (Romans 11:32)

This is not universalism; it is the leveling truth that both Jews and Gentiles are shut up under sin so that salvation is clearly mercy, not merit.

The Doxology: When Theology Becomes Worship

Paul ends where all doctrine should end: worship.

"O the depth of the riches both of the wisdom and knowledge of God!" (Romans 11:33)

Paul is not confused; he is overwhelmed. He has traced the sovereign wisdom of God through Israel's stumbling, Gentile inclusion, remnant preservation, and future restoration. And the only honest conclusion is doxology:

"For of him, and through him, and to him, are all things: to whom be glory for ever. Amen." (Romans 11:36)

This is the final corrective to pride. If everything is "of him," then you are not self-made. If everything is "through him," then you are not self-sustained. If everything is "to him," then you are not the point.

Summary

Romans 11 declares that God has not rejected Israel. He has preserved a remnant by grace, even when the majority stumbled in unbelief. Israel's current hardening is partial and temporary, serving God's purpose of bringing salvation to the Gentiles and provoking Israel toward a future turning.

Gentile believers are grafted into the people of God by faith and must not boast. The root supports the branches, and presumption is spiritually lethal. Paul calls the church to behold both the goodness and severity of God, to continue in faith, and to maintain humility.

The chapter culminates in the revelation that Israel's story is not finished: a future mercy awaits, grounded in God's irrevocable calling. The only fitting response is worship—because God's ways are deeper than human calculation, and His mercy is greater than human failure.

Application

1. Refuse the pride that turns mercy into entitlement

   If Gentiles can be grafted in, Gentiles can also become arrogant. Gratitude is the posture of grace; boasting is the posture of blindness. Never speak as though you "replaced" Israel. You were included.

2. Guard against spiritual calluses

   One of the most frightening themes in Romans 11 is that repeated exposure to truth can harden instead of heal. Habits are good—until habits replace hunger. Ask: has the Word become background noise to me? Has worship become routine without reverence?

3. Continue in kindness: keep faith central, not merely culture

Paul's warning is aimed at institutional religion as much as individual hearts. Churches can preserve forms while losing faith. Keep the gospel central. Keep Scripture authoritative. Keep Christ as the only righteousness.

4. Learn to hope for people who look impossible

If God is able to graft Israel in again, He is able to save the person you think is unreachable. Pray like Paul. Speak like Paul. And leave room for resurrection-level surprises.

5. Let doctrine become doxology

If Romans 11 does not end in worship, you have not truly seen it. The point is not to win arguments about prophecy, but to humble pride, enlarge hope, and magnify mercy—until your theology becomes praise.

Prayer

Father,

You are faithful, and Your Word does not fail. Forgive us for the pride that forgets we stand by grace and not by merit. Deliver us from boasting, and teach us to fear presumption.

Keep our hearts soft under Your Word. Guard us from spiritual calluses—where truth becomes familiar but no longer transforms. Keep Christ central, and keep faith alive, so that we continue in Your kindness and do not settle for the empty comfort of tradition without love.

We pray for Israel, as Paul did: open blind eyes, remove unbelief, and bring many to the Deliverer. And we pray for our own homes, our church, and our community—make us faithful witnesses of the gospel, and make us quick to worship when we see Your wisdom.

We ask this to the Father,

in the name of Jesus. Amen.

Fortress of Justification

24

The Logic of a Living Sacrifice

Romans 12 is not a change of subject; it is the necessary consequence of everything Paul has said so far. The first eleven chapters have established what God has done—His righteousness revealed, His mercy displayed, His Son given, His Spirit granted, His people preserved, His promises secured. Now Paul turns and asks the only honest question left:

If God has done all this for us, what kind of life should follow?

Paul answers with two commands and one goal. He calls believers to (1) present their bodies, (2) reject worldly conformity and pursue inward transformation, so that (3) they can live intelligently and practically in the will of God.

The "Therefore" That Changes Everything

"I beseech you therefore, brethren, by the mercies of God..." (Romans 12:1)

The word "therefore" is a hinge. Paul is not beginning a new book inside the book; he is drawing a conclusion. Romans 12 does not stand on human willpower. It stands on divine mercy.

Paul does not say, "I command you by the fear of punishment." He says, "I urge you by the mercies of God." That means Christian obedience is not powered by terror, guilt manipulation, or the pressure to perform. It is powered by gratitude and astonishment: God has been merciful to the undeserving, and that mercy creates a moral claim on the whole person.

Mercy, in Scripture, is not mere softness. Mercy is God's withholding of what we deserve, and His decision to do good to us anyway. Paul has already said it plainly:

"But God commendeth his love toward us, in that, while we were yet sinners, Christ died for us." (Romans 5:8)

So when Paul says "by the mercies of God," he is gathering up everything—justification, adoption, the Spirit, hope, perseverance, God's unbreakable love, and the promise that nothing can separate us from Him. This "therefore" is built out of grace.

The First Command: Present Your Bodies

"...that ye present your bodies a living sacrifice, holy, acceptable unto God..." *(Romans 12:1)*

Paul's word for "present" is the language of offering. It is not the language of casual volunteering. It is the language of surrender.

And he does not begin with "present your ideas" or "present your intentions." He begins with the body. That is not accidental. The body is where choices become visible—hands, feet, mouth, eyes, time, appetite, energy, schedule, work, relationships. The body is the daily theater of obedience.

A Sacrifice, Not Merely an Offering

In Israel's worship, sacrifices cost something. They were not the leftover margins of life. Paul's point is not that God wants a portion of you; it is that God has rightful claim to you.

Yet Paul says this sacrifice is "living." That is the painful part.

A dead sacrifice is offered once. A living sacrifice must be offered again and again—morning, afternoon, evening; at work, at home; when you feel spiritual and when you do not.

This is where Christian discipleship becomes realistic: the issue is not whether you would die for Christ in one dramatic moment. The issue is whether you will live for Him in a thousand ordinary moments.

Holy and Acceptable

"Holy" means set apart. Your life is no longer owned by personal whim; it is dedicated to God's purposes. "Acceptable" means pleasing—fit for God's use, congruent with His character, aligned with His will.

This is not perfectionism. It is direction. The question is not, "Do I stumble?" The question is, "Who owns me? What direction governs me? Whose purposes am I serving?"

"Reasonable Service": The Logic of Worship

"...which is your reasonable service." (Romans 12:1)

This phrase is one of Paul's most important. The word translated "reasonable" is connected to "logic." Paul is saying: this is the rational conclusion. If Romans 1–11 is true, then Romans 12:1 must follow.

Christian obedience is not a random spiritual hobby added to life; it is the only sane response to grace.

And "service" here is worship-language. Paul is not merely saying, "do religious chores." He is saying that presenting yourself to God is your true worship—not confined to a building, a meeting time, or a ritual. Your worship is your whole life offered to God.

The Second Command: Refuse the World's Mold

"And be not conformed to this world..." (Romans 12:2)

The world does not merely invite; it presses. It has a pattern, a mold, a "schematic" for what a human life should be. The world wants you shaped by its priorities:

- self at the center

- comfort as the goal

- approval as the currency

- pleasure as the compass

- autonomy as the highest good

Paul says: do not let the age press you into that shape.

This is not a call to be strange for its own sake, or abrasive, or socially unaware. It is a call to resist the invisible pressure that quietly normalizes unbelief.

The Alternative: Be Transformed From the Inside Out

"...but be ye transformed by the renewing of your mind..." (Romans 12:2)

"Transformed" is the language of metamorphosis—a change in form and a change in nature that proceeds from within. Paul is not describing superficial adjustment or moral refinement, but a fundamental re-creation of the person. In biological metamorphosis, the caterpillar does not simply improve its habits or learn to crawl more efficiently. It undergoes dissolution. The structures that once defined it are broken down, and from that apparent loss a new creature is formed. What emerges is not a better caterpillar, but something entirely new.

This is the kind of transformation Paul has in view. The Christian life is not outside-in behavior modification, but inside-out renewal. The old patterns are not merely restrained; they are replaced. The believer is being reshaped at the level of identity, desire, and direction.

That transformation happens "by the renewing of your mind." The mind here is not mere intelligence or information intake. It is the believer's operating system—the framework through which reality is interpreted, values are assigned, and decisions are made about what ultimately matters. As that inner framework is renewed by truth, the life that flows from it changes accordingly. Conduct follows conviction. Obedience follows renewal. What God transforms within inevitably reshapes how the believer lives without.

A renewed mind means:

• new definitions of success

• new measures of value

• new instincts about what is good

• new reflexes in temptation

• new priorities in time and money

- new compassion for people

- new fear of sin and new love for holiness

This is why mere external conformity to church culture is never enough. A person can learn Christian vocabulary and still think exactly like the age. Paul is not satisfied with that. He insists on renovation at the level of thought, desire, and judgment.

The Goal: Discern and Live the Will of God

"...that ye may prove what is that good, and acceptable, and perfect, will of God." (Romans 12:2)

"Prove" here is not "prove on a chalkboard." It is test and approve by experience—like examining something, verifying it, and recognizing its genuineness.

Paul is describing a life where the believer becomes increasingly competent at discerning God's will in practice—not by waiting passively for mystical impressions, but by being so renewed that obedience becomes clearer.

God's will is described as:

- good — it truly benefits, even when it costs

- acceptable — pleasing to God, aligned with His character

- perfect — complete, lacking nothing, never half-measures

This is an essential correction for anxious Christians: God's will is not a cruel puzzle designed to trick you. It is good. And as your mind is renewed, you become more able to recognize it and walk in it.

Summary

Romans 12:1–2 is Paul's logical conclusion to the mercies described in Romans 1–11. Because God has saved us by grace, we must respond by presenting ourselves wholly to Him as a living sacrifice. This is not irrational fanaticism; it is reasonable worship.

The Christian life requires resistance to the world's shaping pressure and pursuit of inward transformation through a renewed mind. As the mind is renewed, believers gain practical discernment: they learn to recognize and live out the good, pleasing, and complete will of God.

Application

1. Ask the direct question: Who is your body serving?

   Your hands, your mouth, your eyes, your time, your schedule—these are not neutral. They are instruments. If you belong to Christ, then your body is not your own to spend as you please; it is to be presented.

   A simple daily discipline helps: begin the day with an explicit offering—"Lord, this body is Yours today."

2. Identify the mold that is pressing you

   The world's pressure is rarely dramatic. It is constant. Name it specifically:

   Is it the pressure to be comfortable at all costs?

   The pressure to be liked?

   The pressure to be entertained?

   The pressure to be perpetually outraged?

   The pressure to be autonomous?

   You cannot resist what you refuse to identify.

3. Renew the mind with inputs strong enough to reshape you

   Transformation does not happen by accident. Minds are renewed by steady exposure to truth— Scripture, prayer, worship, and the fellowship of believers.

   If the world gets six days of influence and God gets ten minutes, the mold will win.

4. "Prove" the will of God by practicing what is already clear

   Much paralysis comes from waiting to know everything before obeying anything. Paul's logic is the opposite: obey what is clear, and clarity increases.

   There are commands you do not need special revelation to begin:

   repent, pray, forgive, serve, tell the truth, practice purity, do justice, love your neighbor, share the gospel.

Prayer

Father,

Your mercies have been great toward us. You have loved us when we were unlovable, and You have given Your Son for us when we deserved judgment. Forgive us for living as though Your mercy made no claim on us.

Help us to present our bodies to You—hands, feet, mouth, mind, and time—as a living sacrifice. Deliver us from the world's pressure to fit its mold. Renew our minds by Your Word and by Your Spirit, that we may recognize what pleases You.

Teach us to live intelligently in Your will—what is good, what is acceptable, what is complete. Make us steady, humble, and useful. We ask this to the Father, with the Spirit's help,

in Jesus' name. Amen.

25

The Renewed Mind in Real Life

Romans 12 is Paul's answer to a very practical question: If I am justified by grace, what does a transformed life actually look like on Monday morning? Last week's call to be a "living sacrifice" (12:1–2) is not meant to remain an inspiring slogan. Paul immediately moves from principle to practice. A sacrificed life is not vague spiritual intensity; it is a renewed mind expressed in humility, service, sincere love, unity, and enemy-love.

271

The Renewed Mind Begins With Humility

"For I say, through the grace given unto me, to every man... not to think of himself more highly than he ought to think; but to think soberly..."
(Romans 12:3)

Paul starts where pride is most likely to reappear: spiritual people can become proud of being spiritual. So he calls the church to "think soberly" —to have a mind that has been rescued, recalibrated, and put under the helmet of salvation.

This is not false humility ("I am nothing"), and it is not self-exaltation ("I am everything"). It is sanity: I am what I am by grace. If God had not rescued me, I would still be blind, self-righteous, and enslaved. Therefore I cannot look down on others as though I am the source of my own goodness.

Paul grounds that sobriety in two realities:

• Grace was given (even Paul's ministry rests on received grace, not earned status).

• Faith is measured out (whatever capacity, courage, or ability you have to act in trust toward God is itself a gift).

So the renewed mind is not self-inflated. It is rescued. It is grateful. It is steady.

The Renewed Mind Sees the Church as One Body

*"For as we have many members in one body...
so we, being many, are one body in Christ, and
every one members one of another." (Romans
12:4–5)*

Here Paul changes the whole way believers think
about "church." Church is not a spiritual event you
attend; it is a living organism you belong to. And
belonging means responsibility: members belong to
one another.

Even "small" parts matter. The body can continue
when something is missing, but it will not be whole.
Paul's point is not to flatter the insecure; it is to correct
the independent. The renewed mind does not say, "I
don't need them," or "they don't need me." It says,
"Christ has joined me to them, and my life is now
obligated to their good."

The Renewed Mind Uses Gifts as Stewardship, Not Spotlight

*"Having then gifts differing according to the
grace that is given to us..." (Romans 12:6)*

Paul lists gifts—prophecy, service, teaching,
exhortation, giving, leadership, mercy—and your

emphasis is exactly right: none of these are trophies. They are tools. They are given "according to grace," which means the very thing that could become a reason for boasting is designed to crush boasting.

Paul's repeated logic is simple:

• If it is your gift, use it.

• Use it with the right posture: proportion, sincerity, diligence, cheerfulness.

Scripture provides a sobering warning in the account of Ananias and Sapphira. Their contribution was real money, placed before the apostles and received by the church, yet it was spiritually false. The sin was not that they gave too little, but that they gave deceptively. Their offering was shaped by image rather than integrity, by a desire to appear generous rather than a heart renewed by grace. The external act mimicked devotion, but the inner reality contradicted it.

A renewed mind gives for an entirely different reason. It gives because God has given—freely, truthfully, and without hypocrisy. Such generosity does not manipulate perception or seek control through appearance. It flows from alignment with God's character, where obedience is not performative but sincere, and where worship is measured not by public display, but by faithfulness before God who sees the heart.

The Renewed Mind Produces Love Without Performance

"Let love be without dissimulation..." (Romans 12:9)

Now Paul turns from gifts to character. Gifts can be exercised without love; therefore Paul insists on love that is real.

He describes love with concrete behaviors:

- Moral clarity: hate evil; cling to good.

- Family affection: be devoted; honor one another.

- Eagerness: not lazy in zeal; fervent in spirit; serving the Lord.

- Resilience: rejoicing in hope; patient in tribulation; persistent in prayer.

- Generosity and openness: sharing with saints; practicing hospitality.

Worldly "love" often loves how someone makes me feel or what I can get. That is not love; it is exchange. Christian love is sacrificial. It pours itself out even when nothing is returned.

The Renewed Mind Handles Conflict Inside the Body

"Bless them which persecute you: bless, and curse not." (Romans 12:14)

The Roman church was a mixed congregation with real tension—Jewish believers returning to a Gentile-led church, disagreements about law and liberty, identity and practice. In that setting, Paul's commands are not theoretical:

• Bless the ones who give you a hard time.

• Refuse the spirit of retaliation.

• Learn shared emotional life: rejoice with those who rejoice; weep with those who weep.

• Pursue harmony: different notes, one chord.

Harmony does not require sameness. It requires humility, patience, and a shared center—Christ.

And Paul specifically attacks the "haughty" posture. The renewed mind does not sort the church by importance. It associates with the lowly. It refuses conceit. It treats the smallest as belonging to Christ.

The Renewed Mind Loves Enemies Outside the Body

Here Paul widens the circle. The sacrificed life is not only how you treat your friends at church; it is how you treat your enemies in the world.

- No retaliation: do not repay evil for evil.

- Public integrity: provide things honest in the sight of all.

- Peaceable intent: as much as depends on you, live peaceably.

- No personal vengeance: step aside and let God handle justice.

Get out of the way and let God's wrath have its course. Human vengeance is always inferior—morally, spiritually, and finally. God does not lose the record. Nobody "gets away with it." Either justice is met in Christ for the repentant, or justice is met in judgment for the unrepentant. But justice will be met.

And then Paul goes further: not only refuse vengeance—do active good.

> "If thine enemy hunger, feed him... for in so doing thou shalt heap coals of fire on his head." (Romans 12:20)

It is not petty revenge by kindness; it is an attempt to awaken conscience, to ignite moral reality, to turn an enemy into a neighbor.

The chapter ends with the summary command:

"Be not overcome of evil, but overcome evil with good." (Romans 12:21)

Evil is not only something done against you; it is something that can get into you—reshaping your mind back into the world's pattern: self-centeredness, retaliation, pride, contempt. The renewed mind resists that infection by answering evil with good.

Summary

Romans 12 shows what a "living sacrifice" looks like in daily life. The renewed mind begins with sober humility, recognizes the church as one body, and treats spiritual gifts as stewardship for the good of others. It produces sincere love, practical service, and unity inside the church. It also produces an enemy-loving posture outside the church: refusing revenge, pursuing peace, trusting God's justice, and overcoming evil with good.

Application

1. Check your "saved mind" each morning.

Ask: Am I starting today as a rescued person, or as a self-made person?

2. Treat your gift as an assignment, not an identity.

    Your gift is not proof you are important; it is proof you are responsible.

3. Practice love that costs you something.

    Real love shows up in time, attention, patience, forgiveness, and generosity—not in slogans.

4. Refuse the luxury of retaliation.

    When you repay evil for evil, you don't defeat evil —you spread it. Trust God with justice and answer with good.

5. Aim at harmony, not uniformity.

    Different notes can make one chord, but only if everyone stays in tune with Christ.

Prayer

Father,

Thank You for saving us, not only from judgment, but from the proud and self-centered mind that would have destroyed us.

Give us sober thinking—rescued thinking—so that we do not exalt ourselves, and we do not despise others.

Teach us to serve the body of Christ with the gifts You have given, in sincerity, diligence, and cheerfulness. Make our love real, without hypocrisy. Help us to honor one another, endure trials with hope, and persist in prayer.

And when we are wronged, keep us from vengeance. Help us to live peaceably as far as it depends on us, to trust Your justice, and to overcome evil with good.

in Jesus' name. Amen.

26

Owe No Man Anything: The Christian, the State, the Neighbor, and the Dawn

Romans 13 continues Paul's "therefore" life—what it looks like to live as a living sacrifice with a renewed mind (Romans 12:1–2). It is easy to imagine sacrifice as something mystical, private, and internal. Paul refuses that. He takes the renewed mind and presses it into the most public places a believer lives:

1. our relationship to governing authority (13:1–7),

2. our obligations to neighbors (13:8–10), and

3. our urgency in a world that is running out of night (13:11–14).

The logic of Romans 13 is simple: If Christ is Lord, He is Lord over my politics, my pocketbook, my reputation, my relationships, and my appetites. A sacrificed life is not merely how I feel about Jesus; it is how I obey Jesus where obedience costs.

The Christian and Governing Authority

Paul begins with a hard command:

> *"Let every soul be subject unto the higher powers. For there is no power but of God: the powers that be are ordained of God." (Romans 13:1)*

He does not say, "Be subject when you approve." He says, "Let every soul be subject." And he does not ground the command in the worthiness of rulers, but in the providence of God: "the powers that be are ordained of God."

That immediately raises the objection everyone feels: But what about wicked rulers? What about incompetent rulers? What about rulers who misuse power? Paul is not ignorant of that question. He is writing to Christians in the capital city of the Empire. Whatever else Rome was, it was not a gentle place for the church to live. Yet the apostolic command remains.

Paul's point is not that every ruler is righteous, or that every law is wise, or that every government action is morally pure. His point is something deeper: God is not absent from history. The rise and fall of nations does not mean God has lost control; it means God's purposes are often higher than what we can see.

Scripture is full of this uncomfortable truth:

- Pharaoh sits on his throne, and God uses that throne—even Pharaoh's defiance—to display His own glory.

- Nebuchadnezzar rises, and God uses him as a rod of discipline.

- Cyrus rules as a pagan monarch, and God uses him to open a door no man could have opened.

The lesson is not "rulers are good." The lesson is "God is God." And because God is God, the believer's default posture toward authority is not rebellion, but submission.

Paul continues:

> *"Whosoever therefore resisteth the power, resisteth the ordinance of God: and they that resist shall receive to themselves damnation."* *(Romans 13:2)*

This is not a command to become passive, mindless, or naïve. It is a command to refuse the spirit of lawlessness. Christians are not anarchists. We do not treat society as though order is optional. We are people of a King, and therefore we honor the structure of authority that God has allowed to exist in the world.

Then Paul explains the design of civil government:

> *"For rulers are not a terror to good works, but to the evil." (Romans 13:3)*

The purpose of government is to restrain wrongdoing and commend social good. When government does what it was designed to do, it functions as a kind of common grace—an instrument that makes life livable, families stable, commerce possible, communities safer.

Paul even calls the governing authority "the minister of God":

> *"For he is the minister of God to thee for good." (Romans 13:4)*

That is a stunning phrase. Paul does not say the ruler is a minister of God because the ruler is holy, or because the ruler is saved, or because the ruler loves the truth. He says the ruler is a "minister" in the sense that civil authority is a tool God uses to preserve order in a fallen world.

And then Paul adds a sobering note:

"But if thou do that which is evil, be afraid; for he beareth not the sword in vain: for he is the minister of God, a revenger to execute wrath upon him that doeth evil." (Romans 13:4)

Government possesses coercive power—"the sword." Paul does not pretend that the sword is always wielded perfectly. But he does insist it exists for a reason. A world with no lawful restraint becomes a world where the strong devour the weak.

So Paul gives the conclusion:

"Wherefore ye must needs be subject, not only for wrath, but also for conscience sake." (Romans 13:5)

A believer obeys not merely to avoid punishment, but because conscience is tied to lordship. If Christ is Lord, then I cannot decide that my obedience is optional whenever I am irritated. The renewed mind submits because it fears God more than it fears man —and therefore refuses the lawless spirit that thrives on contempt.

Submission is not the same as surrendering moral discernment.

There is an important balance the church must keep: submission to authority is not the same thing as calling evil good. The Bible never commands Christians to violate conscience or worship the state.

It commands Christians to live peaceably, honorably, and lawfully under civil order as far as they are able.

Paul himself models the distinction. At times he submitted quietly—enduring unjust treatment without retaliation. At other times he used lawful means to appeal, to clarify, and to hold officials accountable within their own legal framework. He did not treat law as meaningless; he treated it as one of the restraining mercies God provides in a broken world.

So Christians are not called to be seditious, but neither are they called to be careless. We are called to be good citizens, not because we worship government, but because we worship God.

Taxes, Revenue, Respect, and Honor

Paul makes the obligations explicit:

> "For for this cause pay ye tribute also: for they are God's ministers, attending continually upon this very thing." (Romans 13:6)

> "Render therefore to all their dues: tribute to whom tribute is due; custom to whom custom; fear to whom fear; honour to whom honour." (Romans 13:7)

It is painful to read those words when you dislike how taxes are spent, or when you feel government wastes what citizens sacrifice to produce. But Paul does not ground taxation in our approval of the budget. He grounds it in conscience and order. Once the obligation is met, the believer releases the outcome to God, who judges rulers and nations perfectly.

Also notice: Paul distinguishes between respecting the office and approving the person. "Honour to whom honour" does not require you to pretend a leader is virtuous. It requires you to refuse contempt, slander, and lawless mockery. The Christian must not become the kind of person whose heart is trained to despise.

The Christian and the Neighbor

After addressing the "big" obligation (the state), Paul turns to the "near" obligation (your neighbor).

> *"Owe no man any thing, but to love one another: for he that loveth another hath fulfilled the law." (Romans 13:8)*

Paul is not primarily giving a lecture on commercial borrowing here. His theme is moral and relational: do not live in unresolved obligation. Do not be the kind of person who lives off what others carry. Pay what you owe—your dues to civic order, your duties in community life, and your debts of love to people around you.

And this is where Christian ethics gets beautifully simple: Paul summarizes the moral law as neighbor-love.

> *"For this, Thou shalt not commit adultery, Thou shalt not kill, Thou shalt not steal, Thou shalt not bear false witness, Thou shalt not covet... Thou shalt love thy neighbour as thyself."* (Romans 13:9)

> *"Love worketh no ill to his neighbour: therefore love is the fulfilling of the law."* (Romans 13:10)

Paul is not abolishing the moral commandments. He is showing what they were aiming at: love that refuses to injure.

- If you truly love your neighbor, you do not exploit his spouse.

- If you truly love your neighbor, you do not destroy his life.

- If you truly love your neighbor, you do not steal his goods.

- If you truly love your neighbor, you do not covet his portion.

This is where the renewed mind becomes visible. The world trains us to see people as obstacles, competitors, tools, or threats. The renewed mind sees people as neighbors—image-bearers who need truth, mercy, stability, and light.

A Christian should never be known as the neighbor who takes, demands, complains, or spreads turmoil. The Christian should be known as the one who is steady, helpful, truthful, peaceable, and generous— not to earn salvation, but because salvation has already claimed the life.

The Christian and the Dawn

Paul closes with urgency. His tone shifts from obligation to alarm clock.

> *"And that, knowing the time, that now it is high time to awake out of sleep: for now is our salvation nearer than when we believed."* *(Romans 13:11)*

Paul does not mean we are not saved. He means the final completion of salvation—resurrection, vindication, fullness, glory—is closer than ever. History is not an endless cycle; it is a storyline moving toward an appointed Day.

> *"The night is far spent, the day is at hand..."* *(Romans 13:12)*

Night is an image for the present age's darkness: ignorance, lust, violence, idolatry, pride, spiritual numbness. Day is the revealing reign of Christ, when darkness will not be tolerated and hidden things will be exposed.

Therefore Paul gives two commands: put off and put on.

Put Off the Works of Darkness

"Let us therefore cast off the works of darkness..." (Romans 13:12)

This is warfare language. The believer is not called to make peace with darkness. We fight it—not by hating our neighbors, but by refusing to live like the darkness has a right to us.

Paul names the kinds of darkness that often dominate societies:

"Let us walk honestly, as in the day; not in rioting and drunkenness, not in chambering and wantonness, not in strife and envying." (Romans 13:13)

Notice the categories:

• Appetites (drunkenness, sensuality)

• Sexual sin (chambering, wantonness)

• Relational corrosion (strife, envying)

These are not "private issues." They poison families, destroy reputations, fracture communities, and harden consciences. Paul is not merely protecting individual morality; he is protecting the witness of the church as a city set on a hill.

Put on the Armor of Light

"...and let us put on the armour of light."
(Romans 13:12)

Light is not merely "truth" in the abstract. Light is a lived testimony—faithfulness, clarity, purity, honesty, courage, humility. Paul pictures the believer as a soldier—not against flesh and blood neighbors, but against darkness that blinds neighbors.

That is why Paul's urgency matters: if the day is approaching, we cannot afford to sleep-walk through our calling. We cannot afford to waste years on petty lusts, petty rivalries, and petty entertainments while souls drift toward judgment.

Put on the Lord Jesus Christ

Paul ends with the most practical command in the chapter:

"But put ye on the Lord Jesus Christ, and make not provision for the flesh, to fulfil the lusts thereof." (Romans 13:14)

To "put on" Christ is clothing language. It is not pretending. It is not a religious costume. It is wrapping your life so tightly in the priorities of Jesus that the cold air of the age stays outside—and the warmth of His life shapes your choices.

And then Paul adds a command with surgical wisdom: make no provision for the flesh. Do not set the table for temptations you say you want to resist. Do not feed the appetite you say you want to starve. Do not stock the pantry of sin and then act surprised when your willpower collapses.

The renewed mind recognizes time. The dawn is coming. Therefore:

- I will not live as though darkness is harmless.

- I will not live as though my neighbors are my enemy.

- I will not live as though Christ's return is distant and theoretical.

- I will put on Christ—today.

Summary

Romans 13 teaches that the sacrificed life is lived publicly and practically. Christians owe lawful submission, taxes, respect, and honor to governing authority as an act of conscience toward God. Christians owe love to their neighbors, because love fulfills the moral law by refusing harm. And Christians must live urgently, because the night is far spent and the Day is near: we must cast off darkness, put on light, put on Christ, and refuse to make provision for the flesh.

Application

1. Practice submission without becoming spiritually passive.

   Be law-abiding, peaceable, and respectful—while keeping your conscience anchored to Christ. Use lawful means wisely when needed, but refuse the spirit of rebellion.

2. Pay your dues with integrity.

   Render what is owed—taxes, revenue, respect, honor—without grumbling that becomes contempt. Leave rulers to answer to God.

3. Be the best neighbor on your road.

Ask: If everyone on this street lived like me, would this neighborhood be safer, kinder, and more stable—or more selfish and tense? Love "works no ill."

4. Live like the dawn is real.

The day is nearer now than when you first believed. Treat time as stewardship. Put off what drags you into darkness; put on what trains you for light.

5. Stop feeding what you're praying to defeat.

"Make no provision for the flesh" means removing predictable sources of temptation. Do not keep inviting the battle you say you want to avoid.

Prayer

Father,

You are Lord over history, Lord over nations, and Lord over our daily lives. Give us hearts that submit with clean consciences, not because rulers are always right, but because You are always God. Teach us to render what we owe with integrity—tribute, honor, respect —without bitterness.

By Your Spirit, form in us a love that does no harm to our neighbors. Make us faithful, peaceable, generous people—lights in the community where You have placed us.

And as the day draws near, wake us from spiritual sleep. Help us to cast off the works of darkness, to put on the armor of light, and to put on the Lord Jesus Christ. Keep us from making provision for the flesh, and make our lives a steady testimony of Your grace.

in Jesus' name. Amen.

Fortress of Justification

27

For His
Good

Paul has been pressing one theme since Romans 12: the justified life becomes a transformed life. The gospel does not merely rescue us from condemnation; it creates in us a new mind—a Christ-centered worldview. And the renewed mind does not stay private. It shows up in relationships.

Romans 14–15 addresses one of the most common threats to church health: not heresy, but prideful conscience—Christians turning personal convictions into weapons.

Paul's aim is not to minimize holiness. It is to protect the church from a holiness that is really self-exaltation, and a liberty that is really self-pleasing.

> "Let every one of us please his neighbour for his good to edification." (Romans 15:2)

That line defines the entire passage: Christian strength exists to build others up.

The Problem: Conscience Conflicts in a Mixed Church

Paul opens:

> "Him that is weak in the faith receive ye, but not to doubtful disputations." (Romans 14:1)

The "weak" here is not weak in saving faith. The issue is weakness of conscience—a believer whose Christian liberty is narrow and whose spiritual safety feels tied to certain restrictions.

In Rome, the tensions were sharpened by Jewish–Gentile friction. Jewish believers carried long-formed habits (dietary scruples, calendar observance). Gentile believers often felt freedom in Christ more immediately. These two groups were not merely "different"; they were tempted to treat each other as inferior.

Paul identifies two common sins that show up whenever convictions differ:

- The strong despise the weak ("How childish. How backward.")

- The weak judge the strong ("How worldly. How careless.")

> *"Let not him that eateth despise him that eateth not; and let not him which eateth not judge him that eateth: for God hath received him." (Romans 14:3)*

Paul's grounding principle is not "everyone's right." It is stronger than that: God has received him. If the Master has welcomed the servant, who are you to treat him as an outsider?

> *"Who art thou that judgest another man's servant? to his own master he standeth or falleth." (Romans 14:4)*

This is not anti-accountability. Paul is not forbidding correction where Scripture is clear. He is forbidding Christians from acting like they are the ultimate tribunal over opinions and disputable matters.

And he says something that kills both pride and fear:

> *"God is able to make him stand." (Romans 14:4)*

Your brother's sanctification is not held together by your criticisms. God can keep His own servants upright.

Paul then applies this to days and diets:

> *"One man esteemeth one day above another: another esteemeth every day alike. Let every man be fully persuaded in his own mind."* *(Romans 14:5)*

That phrase matters: fully persuaded. Don't borrow someone else's conscience. Don't imitate someone else's liberty, or someone else's scruples, while your own heart is uncertain.

The Foundation: We Live and Die Under One Lord

Paul lifts the discussion from food and days to lordship:

> *"For none of us liveth to himself, and no man dieth to himself."* *(Romans 14:7)*

> *"Whether we live therefore, or die, we are the Lord's."* *(Romans 14:8)*

This is decisive: the church is not a club of private lifestyles. It is a people under a King. And because we are the Lord's, we do not treat one another as though we are free to use each other to prove points.

Paul then reminds them of the coming evaluation:

"We shall all stand before the judgment seat of Christ." (Romans 14:10)

This is not terror for the believer, but sobriety. The reality that Christ will evaluate our lives should produce not suspicion toward one another, but carefulness about what we do with our freedom.

"So then every one of us shall give account of himself to God." (Romans 14:12)

This is the end of "I'll manage everyone else." Paul redirects the believer's attention: Your main assignment is your own walk before Christ.

The Rule of Love: Liberty Must Not Injure a Brother

Now Paul states the practical conclusion:

"Let us not therefore judge one another any more: but judge this rather, that no man put a stumblingblock or an occasion to fall in his brother's way." (Romans 14:13)

He does not say, "Never make moral judgments." He says, "Make this judgment: I will not use my freedom to trip my brother."

Paul is clear that, in itself, food is morally neutral:

> "I know, and am persuaded by the Lord Jesus, that there is nothing unclean of itself." (Romans 14:14)

But neutrality does not end the conversation. The issue is love.

> "If thy brother be grieved with thy meat, now walkest thou not charitably." (Romans 14:15)

This is one of the sharpest lines in the section: you can be theologically correct about liberty and still be morally wrong in how you wield it.

Freedom carries responsibility. The stronger believer bears the heavier load.

Paul's concern is not merely interpersonal sensitivity; it is the integrity of the gospel witness:

> "Let not then your good be evil spoken of." (Romans 14:16)

A believer may be within his rights, yet create a scandal that makes outsiders conclude Christianity is callous or arrogant.

Then Paul centers the church's priorities:

"For the kingdom of God is not meat and drink; but righteousness, and peace, and joy in the Holy Ghost." (Romans 14:17)

This is corrective. Churches fracture when they treat secondary matters like primary matters. Paul says: the kingdom is not defined by menus or calendars. It is defined by righteousness (what honors God), peace (what preserves unity), and joy (the Spirit's sustaining delight in Christ).

So he concludes:

"Let us therefore follow after the things which make for peace, and things wherewith one may edify another." (Romans 14:19)

Edification is the standard: Does this build? Does this strengthen? Does this help my brother run his race?

Paul's final line in the chapter is the conscience principle:

"And he that doubteth is damned if he eat... for whatsoever is not of faith is sin." (Romans 14:23)

In other words: even if the action is morally permissible, if you cannot do it with a clean conscience before God, do not do it. God is not honored by a liberty that is exercised as inner rebellion.

The Strong Must Carry the Weak

Paul begins chapter 15 with a direct assignment:

"We then that are strong ought to bear the infirmities of the weak, and not to please ourselves." (Romans 15:1)

The strong do not get to say, "I'm free, so it doesn't matter." In the church, strength is not a badge; it is a burden. It exists for service.

Then comes the key line:

"Let every one of us please his neighbour for his good to edification." (Romans 15:2)

This instruction must be carefully guarded against people-pleasing. Paul is not commanding codependency. He establishes a clear boundary: for his good—that is, what strengthens righteousness and faith, not what indulges immaturity or empowers sin.

And then Paul anchors it in Christ:

"For even Christ pleased not himself..." (Romans 15:3)

Jesus' thirst at the well provides a striking illustration of this principle. He experiences real fatigue and real bodily need, yet His physical desire yields to the spiritual need set before Him. That is the pattern Scripture sets forth. Christ did not use His rights to insulate Himself from inconvenience or discomfort. He exercised His strength for the sake of others, placing redemptive purpose above personal relief and modeling a life ordered by love rather than self-preservation.Paul also shows that this posture is taught throughout Scripture:

> *"For whatsoever things were written aforetime were written for our learning, that we through patience and comfort of the scriptures might have hope." (Romans 15:4)*

The Word trains endurance and comfort—precisely what church life requires when Christians differ.

Then Paul's desired outcome:

> *"That ye may with one mind and one mouth glorify God..." (Romans 15:6)*

This is not uniformity. It is harmony—many notes, one key. The goal is not that everyone's conscience looks identical, but that everyone's worship rises together without contempt.

So the command becomes:

"Wherefore receive ye one another, as Christ also received us to the glory of God." (Romans 15:7)

Christ did not receive us because we were polished. He received us by grace. And grace received must become grace extended.

The Broader Horizon: A United Church for a Global Gospel

Paul widens the frame. The church's unity is not merely for "getting along." It is for mission.

He shows that Christ's work unites Jew and Gentile so the nations can glorify God, and he stacks Old Testament quotations to prove that this was always God's plan. Then he pours a pastoral blessing:

"Now the God of hope fill you with all joy and peace in believing…" (Romans 15:13)

We often "forget to believe" in the moment. Not losing salvation—losing perspective. When we grip the rope of hope again, joy and peace return. And as hope rises, unity strengthens, because anxious Christians become quarrelsome Christians—but hopeful Christians become steady Christians.

Paul then closes with a window into his own heart: he wants to preach Christ where Christ is not named; he wants to go to Spain; he is carrying an offering to Jerusalem; he is asking for prayer; and he ends as a shepherd:

"Now the God of peace be with you all. Amen."
(Romans 15:33)

That is the tone of the entire section: peace, not point-scoring.

Summary

Romans 14–15 teaches that Christians must not divide over disputable matters of conscience. The strong must not despise; the weak must not judge. We all live and die under one Lord and will all give account to Him. Therefore, liberty must be governed by love: we pursue peace and edification, refusing to use our freedom in ways that wound a brother's conscience. Christ is the model—He did not please Himself. The goal is unity in Christ, harmony in worship, and a church strong enough to carry the gospel outward.

Application

1. Identify the category before you react.

Is the issue clear biblical command, or disputable conscience? Treat the first with firmness; treat the second with charity.

2. Refuse both contempt and judgment.

    If you have liberty, don't sneer. If you have scruples, don't condemn. God receives His servants.

3. Let love put guardrails on your freedom.

    Ask: Will this help my brother run his race—or trip him? Liberty that harms is liberty misused.

4. Obey your conscience—and educate it.

    Never violate conscience "to be mature." But also keep feeding conscience with Scripture so it grows toward biblical clarity.

5. Make "edification" your standard.

    "Please your neighbor" means serve his spiritual good. Sometimes that is gentleness; sometimes that is patient correction; often it is restraint.

6. Remember what the kingdom actually is.

    Not food and drink—righteousness, peace, and joy in the Holy Ghost. Don't turn church life into a contest over secondary matters.

Prayer

Father,

Thank You for receiving us by grace when we did not deserve welcome. Give us the mind of Christ, so we will not despise Your servants or judge them over matters where You have not spoken with strictness. Teach us to honor conscience without making conscience a throne.

Make the strong patient and protective. Strengthen the weak without shaming them. Help us pursue righteousness, peace, and joy in the Holy Ghost. Give us unity in accordance with Christ, so that with one voice we may glorify You.

Fill us with joy and peace in believing, and cause us to abound in hope by the power of the Holy Spirit. We pray to the Father, with the Spirit's help,

in Jesus' name. Amen.

Fortress of Justification

28

The
People the
Gospel Makes

After fifteen chapters of sustained theological argument, ethical exhortation, and pastoral instruction, Paul closes his Epistle to the Romans in a way that often surprises modern readers. Instead of a final summary of doctrine, a recapitulation of justification, or a climactic appeal, he offers a long list of names—men and women, Jews and Gentiles, servants and patrons, leaders and laborers.

Romans 16 is not an appendix. It is the evidence.

What Paul places before us here is the living proof that justification by faith is not an abstract doctrine but a generative power. The gospel Paul has defended, explained, and applied has already produced something tangible: a people.

Commended Servants

Paul begins with Phoebe:

> *"I commend unto you Phebe our sister, which is a servant of the church which is at Cenchrea:*
>
> *That ye receive her in the Lord, as becometh saints, and that ye assist her in whatsoever business she hath need of you: for she hath been a succourer of many, and of myself also."* *(Romans 16:1-2)*

Phoebe is identified not by charisma or title, but by faithful usefulness. She is a servant of the church and a helper of many. The same gospel that strips humanity of boasting (Romans 3) restores dignity to service. Justification does not produce spectators; it produces reliable saints.

That Paul entrusts this letter—his most carefully reasoned exposition of the gospel—to Phoebe is no small detail. Romans is not carried by an apostle, but by a faithful servant. The gospel advances not merely through proclamation, but through trust.

Courageous Co-Laborers

Next Paul greets Priscilla and Aquila:

"Who have for my life laid down their own necks: unto whom not only I give thanks, but also all the churches of the Gentiles." (Romans 16:3–5)

Here Romans 8 becomes flesh. Nothing can separate believers from the love of Christ, and therefore they are freed to risk themselves for one another. The love that justified them now governs their priorities. Their home becomes a church, their lives a shield for the apostle, their faith a quiet bulwark for the gospel.

Justification produces courage—not bravado, but sacrificial loyalty.

A New Social World

The long list that follows is deliberate. Paul names Jews and Gentiles, men and women, slaves and freedmen, households and individuals. No one is ranked. No one is elevated above the others. Each is greeted "in the Lord."

Here is Romans 3 and Romans 10 lived out:

"There is no difference."

This is not sameness. It is unity without hierarchy. The gospel has not erased distinction, but it has erased superiority. Worth is no longer measured by heritage, status, or visibility, but by belonging to Christ.

Paul repeatedly commends labor, endurance, and love—not prominence. The fortress of justification is not built by celebrities, but by faithful stones set quietly in place.

Guarded Unity

After warmth comes warning:

> *"Mark them which cause divisions and offences contrary to the doctrine which ye have learned; and avoid them." (Romans 16:17)*

Unity does not mean indiscretion. The same gospel that creates patience with the weak (Romans 14–15) requires resistance to deception. Smooth words that distort the gospel threaten the entire structure.

Yet the warning ends with promise:

> *"The God of peace shall bruise Satan under your feet shortly." (Romans 16:20)*

The church does not guard the gospel alone. The God who justified them will defend what He has built. The ancient promise of Genesis 3 echoes here: the people of God, grounded in Christ, will stand victorious.

Glory as the Goal

Paul closes where he began:

"Now to him that is of power to stablish you according to my gospel...

To God only wise, be glory through Jesus Christ for ever. Amen." (Romans 16:25&27)

The gospel was not improvised. It was revealed for obedience, proclaimed among all nations, and aimed at forming a faithful people who glorify God. Justification is not the end of God's purpose—it is the foundation upon which everything else stands.

Summary

Romans 16 shows us the finished architecture of justification by faith:

• A people marked by service rather than status

• Courage shaped by love for Christ

• Unity without hierarchy

• Discernment without hostility

• Faithfulness lived in ordinary relationships

This is what the gospel builds when it is believed.

Application

We are reminded that the strength of the church is not found in novelty, influence, or visibility, but in quiet faithfulness. The gospel does not ask us to be extraordinary; it calls us to be dependable.

Justification places us within a people. It gives us names, relationships, responsibilities, and accountability. We are stones set into a living structure—not to draw attention to ourselves, but to support one another and bear the weight of glory.

The question Romans leaves us with is not merely whether we understand the gospel, but whether we are becoming the kind of people it produces.

Prayer

Father,

We thank You for the gospel that not only forgives sinners but forms a people.

Thank You for faithful servants, courageous laborers, and quiet saints whose lives testify to Your grace.

Establish us in Christ, guard us in truth, and make us useful to one another.

May our lives, together, bring glory to You through Jesus Christ our Lord.

Amen.

The Righteousness of God Revealed: Character Before Imputation

One of the most theologically dense and frequently misunderstood phrases in the Epistle to the Romans appears at the very outset of Paul's argument:

"For therein is the righteousness of God revealed from faith to faith" (Rom. 1:17).

Because Romans will later speak explicitly of righteousness being reckoned or imputed to the believer (Rom. 4:3–6), many readers instinctively assume that "the righteousness of God" in Romans 1 must already refer to that imputed righteousness. While understandable, that assumption collapses the careful architecture of Paul's argument and obscures the force of the gospel he proclaims.

This appendix exists to clarify what Paul means—and does not mean—by "the righteousness of God" in Romans 1, and to explain why recognizing this distinction strengthens rather than weakens the doctrine of justification by faith.

1. Revelation Precedes Application

Paul's language in Romans 1 is unmistakably declarative:

"The righteousness of God is revealed..."

The verb is passive and revelatory, not transactional. Paul does not say that righteousness is given, credited, or imputed in this verse. He says it is revealed—unveiled, displayed, made known.

This matters because revelation answers a different question than imputation.

- Imputation asks: How can sinners be counted righteous?

- Revelation asks: What kind of God is acting in the gospel?

Romans 1 answers the second question first. Before Paul explains how righteousness is accounted to believers, he establishes that the God revealed in the gospel is Himself righteous—faithful to His character, just in His judgments, and consistent in His saving work.

2. God's Righteousness as His Moral Consistency

In Scripture, the "righteousness of God" often refers not to something God gives, but to something God is. It describes His unwavering commitment to what is right, His fidelity to His own holiness, and His justice in both judgment and salvation.

In Romans 1, this righteousness is revealed precisely because the gospel addresses a real problem: human unrighteousness under divine wrath (Rom. 1:18). The gospel does not deny God's justice; it displays it. It does not suspend righteousness for the sake of mercy; it satisfies righteousness through Christ.

If God were to justify sinners without first demonstrating His own righteousness, the gospel would appear arbitrary—merciful, perhaps, but unjust. Paul will later insist that God set forth Christ as a propitiation:

"To declare his righteousness... that he might be just, and the justifier of him which believeth in Jesus" (Rom. 3:25–26).

That declaration presupposes that God's righteousness has already been established as the moral foundation of the gospel itself.

3. Why Imputation Cannot Come First

If Romans 1 were read primarily as a statement about imputed righteousness, Paul's argument would unravel.

Imputation answers how sinners are justified—but justification itself requires a prior demonstration that God is righteous in justifying them. Otherwise, forgiveness would appear to be divine leniency rather than divine justice fulfilled.

Paul's progression is deliberate:

1. God is righteous (revealed in the gospel)

2. Humanity is unrighteous (exposed under wrath)

3. Christ satisfies divine righteousness (through the cross)

4. Righteousness is credited to believers (by faith)

To reverse that order is not merely a theological preference; it is an exegetical mistake.

4. Faith Does Not Create Righteousness—It Receives It

When Paul says that God's righteousness is revealed "from faith to faith," he is not describing faith as the source of righteousness, but as the means by which it is perceived, embraced, and trusted.

Faith does not manufacture righteousness.

Faith does not redefine righteousness.

Faith receives what God has already revealed Himself to be.

This preserves the objectivity of the gospel. The good news does not depend on the intensity of human belief but on the unchanging righteousness of God, demonstrated decisively in Jesus Christ.

5. This Reading Does Not Deny Imputation—It Grounds It

Nothing in this reading undermines the later doctrine of imputed righteousness. On the contrary, it protects it.

Romans 4 will speak explicitly of righteousness being "counted" apart from works. Romans 5 will describe believers as being constituted righteous through

Christ. Those truths remain untouched and unthreatened.

But they rest on a prior truth: God does not impute righteousness by suspending justice, but by fulfilling it.

The gospel is not merely that sinners are declared righteous, but that God remains righteous while doing so.

Conclusion

Romans does not begin with the gift of righteousness, but with the revelation of a righteous God. Only once that foundation is laid can Paul unfold the miracle of justification by faith.

To read Romans 1 this way is not to diminish the gospel—it is to preserve its integrity. The fortress stands because its foundation is firm. The good news saves because it reveals a God who is righteous in judgment, faithful to His promises, and just in justifying the ungodly through Christ.

The Wrath of God as Present Judgment and Judicial Abandonment

One of the most arresting claims in the opening chapters of Romans is Paul's insistence that the wrath of God is not merely a future reality, but a present revelation:

> *"For the wrath of God is revealed from heaven against all ungodliness and unrighteousness of men..." (Rom. 1:18).*

For many readers, this language is unsettling. Wrath is commonly understood as something reserved for the final judgment—hell, condemnation, and eschatological punishment. When Paul speaks of wrath as already being revealed, it raises urgent questions: In what sense is God's wrath present now? Is God actively causing sin? How does this relate to human responsibility?

This appendix exists to clarify what Paul means by present wrath, what he does not mean, and why this concept is essential to understanding both judgment and grace in Romans.

1. Revelation, Not Mere Prediction

Paul does not say that the wrath of God will be revealed, though that is certainly true elsewhere. He says it is revealed. The tense matters.

Just as the righteousness of God is revealed in the gospel (Rom. 1:17), the wrath of God is revealed in history. Both are manifestations of God's righteous character. Wrath is not an emotional outburst waiting in the future; it is the present moral response of a holy God to ongoing ungodliness.

This does not replace future judgment. It explains why future judgment will be just.

2. Wrath Expressed as "Giving Over"

The dominant way Paul describes present wrath in Romans 1 is not through catastrophe or direct punishment, but through a repeated phrase:

"Wherefore God also gave them up..." (Rom. 1:24)

"For this cause God gave them up..." (Rom. 1:26)

"God gave them over to a reprobate mind..." (Rom. 1:28)

This language is crucial. God's wrath is revealed not primarily by forcing humanity into sin, but by withdrawing restraint and allowing rebellion to run its course.

This is **judicial abandonment.**

God does not implant evil desires. He removes the barriers that were restraining desires already chosen. The punishment fits the crime: those who insist on autonomy are given what autonomy inevitably produces.

Wrath, in this sense, is God honoring human rebellion with its consequences.

3. Divine Sovereignty Without Moral Causation

A common misunderstanding is to assume that if God "gives people over," He must therefore be morally responsible for what follows. Paul allows no such conclusion.

Throughout Romans 1, the direction of desire is clear:

- Humanity suppresses truth

- Humanity exchanges God's glory

- Humanity refuses gratitude

- Humanity rejects God's knowledge

Only after these acts does God "give them over."

Wrath does not initiate rebellion; it ratifies it.

God's sovereignty is expressed not by coercing sin, but by judging it in a way consistent with human choice. This preserves both divine holiness and human responsibility.

4. Why This Form of Wrath Is So Severe

Judicial abandonment may appear less dramatic than immediate punishment, but Scripture presents it as one of the most terrifying forms of judgment.

To be "given over" is to lose:

- moral clarity,

- proper desire,

- sound judgment,

- and eventually the ability to recognize evil as evil.

This explains why Paul's catalogue of sins ends not merely with wrongdoing, but with approval of wrongdoing (Rom. 1:32). The final stage of wrath is not ignorance, but inversion—where conscience no longer warns but applauds.

Such wrath is severe precisely because it feels like freedom.

5. Present Wrath and Future Judgment Belong Together

Recognizing present wrath does not eliminate future judgment; it explains it.

Romans 2 will speak of:

> *"the day of wrath and revelation of the righteous judgment of God" (Rom. 2:5).*

The same righteousness governs both. Present wrath shows that God already judges sin truthfully. Final judgment will simply make that truth inescapable.

In this way, present wrath is not an alternative to final judgment—it is a preview of it.

6. Why the Gospel Must Be Set Against Present Wrath

The gospel does not rescue sinners merely from future punishment. It rescues them from a present condition of abandonment, blindness, and moral decay.

If wrath were only future, grace would appear optional.

Because wrath is already revealed, grace is urgent.

The gospel interrupts a trajectory already moving toward destruction. It does not merely cancel a sentence; it restores the sinner to God's rule, God's truth, and God's life.

Conclusion

When Paul declares that the wrath of God is revealed from heaven, he is not portraying a volatile deity or excusing human evil. He is describing a righteous God who judges sin by allowing it to bear its own bitter fruit.

This form of wrath vindicates God's justice, preserves human responsibility, and explains why salvation must be more than advice or reform. Humanity does not need mild correction—it needs rescue from a judgment already underway.

Only against the backdrop of present wrath can the gospel be seen for what it truly is: not a soothing message, but a saving intervention by a righteous God.

Judgment According to Works and the Necessity of Paul's Order

Few statements in Romans unsettle modern readers more than Paul's repeated insistence that God judges "according to works":

> *"Who will render to every man according to his deeds" (Rom. 2:6).*

> *"Tribulation and anguish, upon every soul of man that doeth evil..." (Rom. 2:9).*

> *"But glory, honour, and peace, to every man that worketh good..." (Rom. 2:10).*

For readers trained to associate salvation exclusively with faith and grace, this language can sound dangerously close to works-based righteousness. Some rush to soften it. Others attempt to bypass it entirely. Paul does neither.

This appendix exists to explain why Paul speaks this way, what he means by judgment according to works, and why this concept is not a contradiction of justification by faith—but a necessary foundation for it.

1. Paul States the Principle Without Qualification

Paul does not introduce judgment according to works as a hypothetical, an exaggeration, or a rhetorical trap. He presents it as a settled reality grounded in God's righteousness.

- God judges according to truth (Rom. 2:2).

- God shows no partiality (Rom. 2:11).

- God renders to each according to deeds (Rom. 2:6).

This principle is not unique to Romans. It echoes the Old Testament, the teaching of Jesus, and the wider witness of Scripture. Paul is not innovating; he is insisting that God's judgment is morally coherent.

Before Paul explains how sinners are saved, he must establish how God judges.

2. Judgment According to Works Is About Evidence, Not Currency

The key to understanding this section is recognizing what works do in judgment.

Works are not presented as the means by which righteousness is earned. They are presented as the evidence of what a person truly serves, trusts, and loves.

- Works reveal allegiance.

- Works expose the heart.

- Works testify to the direction of a life.

Paul is not describing a balance scale where good deeds outweigh bad deeds. He is describing a courtroom where deeds bear witness. Judgment according to works means that God's verdict corresponds to reality. No one is condemned or vindicated on the basis of profession alone.

This preserves the integrity of judgment. A God who judged apart from evidence would not be righteous.

3. Why Paul Delays the Explanation of Grace

One of the most important features of Romans is when Paul explains justification by faith.

He does not introduce it in Romans 2.

He does not soften judgment in Romans 2.

He allows the weight of judgment to stand.

This delay is intentional.

If Paul were to explain grace before establishing judgment according to works, grace would appear as an escape hatch rather than a rescue. The reader would never feel the full force of the problem grace solves.

Paul must first silence every excuse:

- Moral comparison fails.

- Religious possession fails.

- Ethnic privilege fails.

- Knowledge of the law fails.

Only when every mouth is stopped (Rom. 3:19) can justification be understood as grace rather than indulgence.

4. Works and the Final Judgment of Believers

Some readers fear that judgment according to works introduces insecurity for believers. Paul does not share that concern.

Later in Romans, Paul will make clear that those who are justified by faith are united to Christ, transformed by the Spirit, and brought into a new realm of life. Their works do not create their standing—but they do reflect it.

Judgment according to works does not ask, *Did you earn righteousness?*

It asks, *Did your life bear witness to the righteousness you claimed?*

This is why Paul can affirm both:

- justification by faith apart from works, and

- judgment according to works without contradiction.

Faith unites a person to Christ. Works reveal whether that union is real.

5. Why Paul Refuses to Let Anyone Escape Early

Romans 2 is deliberately uncomfortable because it removes every premature refuge.

The moral man cannot say, "At least I am not like them."

The religious man cannot say, "I possess the truth."

The Jew cannot say, "I have the law."

The Gentile cannot say, "I did not know."

Judgment according to works exposes the common condition of all humanity: knowing enough to be accountable, yet failing to live in accordance with that knowledge.

Only after this exposure does Paul reveal the astonishing truth that God justifies the ungodly—not by ignoring judgment, but by satisfying it through Christ.

Conclusion

Judgment according to works is not the enemy of the gospel. It is the reason the gospel is necessary.

Paul insists on this principle because God is righteous. He judges truthfully, impartially, and in accordance with reality. Works do not purchase salvation, but they do testify. They do not create righteousness, but they do reveal allegiance.

By establishing judgment according to works first, Paul ensures that justification by faith will be understood not as a loophole, but as grace— undeserved, costly, and secure.

Appendix C

Only when judgment stands firm can mercy be truly seen as mercy.

Why Paul Makes the Reader Wait for the Cross

One of the most striking features of the Epistle to the Romans is not what Paul says, but when he says it. For a letter so often used to explain the gospel, Romans delays explicit discussion of the cross and justification far longer than many modern readers expect.

Paul announces the gospel in Romans 1. He declares its power. He insists that it reveals the righteousness of God. And then—rather than moving quickly to Christ's saving work—he spends nearly three chapters exposing sin, judgment, wrath, and human accountability.

This appendix exists to explain why Paul structures his argument this way, and why delaying the cross is not a failure of pastoral sensitivity, but a necessary act of theological faithfulness.

1. Paul Does Not Assume the Problem—He Proves It

Modern gospel presentations often begin with the solution. Paul does not.

He does not assume that his readers already understand the depth of the human problem. Instead, he demonstrates it—carefully, relentlessly, and comprehensively.

- Romans 1 exposes ungodliness and unrighteous-ness.

- Romans 2 dismantles moral comparison and religious confidence.

- Romans 3 silences every remaining defense.

Paul is not slow because he is uncertain. He is deliberate because misdiagnosis produces shallow faith. Until humanity's condition is fully exposed, the cross will be misunderstood—not as rescue, but as embellishment.

2. Premature Grace Produces False Security

If Paul were to introduce the cross before judgment has been firmly established, grace would be heard as permission rather than salvation.

Without the weight of wrath:

- Forgiveness feels unnecessary.

- Justification sounds theoretical.

- Faith becomes a preference rather than a refuge.

Paul refuses to offer comfort before truth has done its work. He does not want readers to agree with the gospel; he wants them to need it.

The delay of the cross is pastoral wisdom. It prevents readers from hiding behind religious familiarity or moral comparison while assuming safety they do not possess.

3. The Cross Must Answer a Real Verdict

Paul's argument is not merely that people sin, but that God is righteous in judging sin. Until that righteousness is established, the cross cannot be rightly understood.

The cross is not:

- God overlooking sin

- God changing His standards

- God suspending justice

It is God satisfying justice.

But satisfaction only makes sense if judgment is real, deserved, and unavoidable. By delaying the cross, Paul ensures that when Christ is finally presented as propitiation, the reader understands what He is answering.

4. Silence Creates Hunger

There is a rhetorical wisdom in Paul's restraint.

As Romans progresses, the reader feels the pressure mounting:

- The road leads only to judgment.

- Every refuge collapses.

- Every mouth is stopped.

By the time Paul reaches "But now..." in Romans 3:21, the reader is no longer curious. He is desperate.

The cross is not introduced casually. It arrives as relief after suffocation, light after darkness, solid ground after the edge of the cliff. Paul does not rush the moment because he wants it to land with full force.

5. Delaying the Cross Honors Its Cost

A cross introduced too early becomes sentimental. A cross introduced too late becomes unbelievable. Paul introduces it at precisely the right moment—when the reader understands that nothing else can stand.

The delay honors:

- the seriousness of sin,
- the righteousness of God,
- the necessity of judgment,
- and the costliness of grace.

Christ does not die to make bad people better, but to rescue condemned people who cannot escape by any other means.

Conclusion

Paul delays the cross because the gospel is not good advice—it is good news. And good news only makes sense when the bad news is fully told.

By forcing the reader to walk the road of judgment without shortcuts, Paul ensures that when Christ is finally revealed as Savior, He is seen not as an accessory to moral improvement, but as the only refuge God has provided.

The delay is not cruelty.

It is mercy.

Appendix D

Only those who have nowhere left to stand will cling to the cross with gratitude, humility, and lasting faith.

Glossary

Apostleship

The divine calling and commissioning by Jesus Christ to proclaim the gospel with authority. In Romans, apostleship is rooted in grace and ordered toward the obedience of faith among all nations, not personal status or control.

Boasting

Any confidence grounded in human achievement, heritage, law-keeping, or moral comparison. Paul excludes boasting because justification rests entirely on God's action, not human merit.

Calling

God's sovereign act of summoning sinners into Christ. Calling establishes identity and belonging prior to obedience and apart from personal qualification.

Circumcision (Outward)

The physical covenant sign given to Israel. In Romans 2, outward circumcision without obedience becomes grounds for judgment rather than security.

Circumcision of the Heart

An inward work of God producing true covenant faithfulness. It is defined by the Spirit, not the letter, and receives praise from God rather than men.

Conscience

The internal witness to moral truth present in all humanity. Conscience does not save or justify; it accuses or excuses and thereby confirms accountability before God.

Covenant

God's binding relationship with His people, grounded in promise and faithfulness. Possession of covenant signs does not negate covenant responsibility.

Deeds / Works

The outward actions that reveal a person's true allegiance and heart direction. Works function as evidence in judgment, not as currency for earning righteousness.

Drawbridge of Faith

A metaphor for Romans 1:16–17, describing faith as the necessary crossing point into the fortress of the gospel. Faith does not generate salvation but connects the sinner to God's saving power.

Faith

Trusting reliance on God as He has revealed Himself in Christ. Faith receives righteousness; it does not create it. The righteous live by faith from beginning to end.

Gatehouse of the Gospel

A metaphor for Romans 1:1–7, where authority, identity, and access are established. Entry into the fortress is defined by Christ's lordship, not by heritage or performance.

Gospel

God's authoritative announcement concerning His Son, Jesus Christ. The gospel reveals God's righteousness, exposes human unrighteousness, and accomplishes salvation through Christ.

Grace

God's unearned favor that restores sinners to rightful allegiance under Christ's lordship. Grace does not exempt from obedience; it produces it.

Imputed Righteousness

The reckoning of righteousness to the believer by faith. In Romans, this doctrine appears after God's own righteousness has been fully established and vindicated.

Judicial Abandonment

A form of present divine wrath in which God "gives over" sinners to the consequences of their chosen rebellion. God does not cause sin but removes restraint, allowing sin to bear its fruit.

Justification

God's judicial declaration that a sinner is righteous on the basis of Christ's work, received by faith. Justification is grounded in God's righteousness, not human achievement.

Judgment According to Works

God's righteous evaluation of humanity based on deeds as evidence of allegiance. This judgment exposes guilt universally and prepares the way for justification by faith.

Law

God's revealed moral will. The law exposes sin, silences excuses, and renders the whole world accountable, but it cannot justify.

Law Written on the Heart

The moral awareness present even among those without the written law. It confirms accountability rather than providing a means of salvation.

Patronage

A Roman social system of status, obligation, and earned favor. Paul dismantles this framework by redefining standing before God entirely by grace.

Peace with God

The settled condition of reconciliation produced by justification. Peace is the result of grace, not the reward of performance.

Propitiation

Christ's sacrificial work that satisfies God's righteous wrath against sin. Propitiation demonstrates that God remains just while justifying sinners.

Righteousness of God

Primarily God's own righteous character—His justice, faithfulness, and moral consistency—revealed in the gospel. Only after this is established does Paul unfold righteousness credited to believers.

Road

A recurring metaphor for humanity's moral trajectory toward judgment. Remaining on the road leads inevitably to condemnation unless one turns to God's provided refuge.

Wrath of God

God's righteous response to sin, revealed both presently (through abandonment) and finally (in judgment). Wrath vindicates God's holiness and makes salvation necessary.

Works of the Law

Human attempts to achieve righteousness through obedience. Paul insists that no flesh is justified by works of the law.

This glossary is intended to be read alongside the argument of the book, not as a substitute for it. Terms derive their full meaning from their place within Paul's unfolding logic in Romans.

About Fireproof Commentaries

Fireproof Commentaries exists to serve pastors, teachers, and believers laboring faithfully in churches that often lack access to extensive resources. Founded out of decades of ministry in small and underserved congregations, Fireproof Commentaries is committed to producing biblically rigorous, Christ-centered studies that strengthen the church without assuming academic training, institutional support, or cultural influence. The aim is not novelty, but clarity— helping readers follow the structure, logic, and force of Scripture as it stands.

Each volume is built on the conviction that Scripture is best understood when its argument is allowed to unfold in order, its tensions are faced honestly, and its conclusions are received on God's terms. Fireproof Commentaries emphasizes theological depth without abstraction, pastoral seriousness without sentimentality, and accessibility without simplification, equipping readers to stand securely in the gospel and to serve faithfully where God has placed them.

www.ingramcontent.com/pod-product-compliance
Lightning Source LLC
Chambersburg PA
CBHW060404130626
46555CB00005B/1990